'Gill is a wit and a charmer. Even when he's wrong, he's superbly full of himself' – Lynn Barber

'One of the finest writers of our time' – Andrew Neil

'A shining intellectual with a remarkable wit. There will never be anyone like him' – Joan Collins

'He never once produced a boring sentence or a phrase that did not shine' – John Witherow

'A true master of the *bon mot*' – Sam Leith

Uncle Dysfunctional

Also by AA Gill

Non-Fiction
AA Gill Is Away
The Angry Island
Previous Convictions
Breakfast at the Wolseley
Table Talk
Paper View
Here and There
AA Gill is Further Away
The Golden Door
Pour Me
Lines in the Sand

Fiction
Sap Rising
Starcrossed

A A GILL

Uncompromising Answers to Life's Most Painful Problems

CANONGATE

Published in Great Britain in 2017 by Canongate Books Ltd,
14 High Street, Edinburgh EH1 1TE

www.canongate.co.uk

2

British Library Cataloguing-in-Publication Data
A catalogue record for this book is available on
request from the British Library

ISBN 978 1 78689 183 9

Typeset in Baskerville and Sentinel by
Palimpsest Book Production Limited, Falkirk, Stirlingshire

Printed and bound in Great Britain by Clays Ltd, St Ives plc.

Introduction by Alex Bilmes

He wasn't a cuddly uncle. His wasn't a reassuring arm around a heaving shoulder, a fond pinch of a tear-stained cheek. There was no coin mysteriously conjured from behind your ear, to be spent on an illicit bag of sweets. He wasn't indulgent. There was no soft touch. He wouldn't tolerate selfishness, or showing off, or self-regard, the musty stink of complacent, old-style masculinity. He was as likely to sneer and scorn as smile and sympathise. You didn't come to him for affirmation, or absolution. You came to be challenged, to have your preconceptions overturned, your follies exposed. You came when you were desperate, and you got what you deserved: strong medicine, in dangerous doses. The effect was immediate. The effect was sobering. The effect was magic.

Yes, he had a filthy tongue and a dirty mind. Your mother might not approve. (For God's sake, don't give this book to your mother.) But he could be empathetic, and compassionate too. He was AA Gill and he wasn't: he was Uncle Dysfunctional, Adrian's id unleashed. He was a performance, an act of outrageous ventriloquism, an uproarious work of fiction that was also true. He was always deadly serious, and he was never not taking the piss.

Uncle Dysfunctional was my idea, Adrian Gill my first marquee signing when, by what he seldom failed to remind me must have been some cosmic clerical error, I was appointed editor of British *Esquire* at the end of 2010. By then, we'd worked together for close to a decade and during that time he had become more than a colleague. He was a friend, and he was a mentor. He was older than me. He'd seen more, done more, lived more, and thought harder and longer than me about what it means to be a man in the world, about what it means to be a father, a son, a lover, a brother, a friend. He advised me, he admonished me, he educated me, and he made me laugh.

And I thought that that was what he should do for the readers of *Esquire*, what he should be for them (and now you) too: a rogue relation, cleverer and braver, wiser and worldlier than us, also madder, and much more difficult. And funnier. Before anything else, he was funny.

Adrian went for it straight away. He loved the silly name. Even over the phone, as I proposed the idea to him, I fancied I could see the gleam in his eye. For those who have somehow never encountered his work before – *really?* – Adrian was, until his death in December 2016, at the age of sixty-two, perhaps the most famous newspaper writer in Britain, the hypodermic-sharp critic and feature writer for the *Sunday Times*, celebrated for his merciless skewerings of second-rate restaurants and his joyful demolitions of terrible TV shows, as well as for his kaleidoscopic travel writing and his unflinching dispatches from some of the world's most benighted places. Simply put, he was one of Fleet Street's all-time greats, inimitable, with a voice and a style and a persona utterly his own.

I knew, because of all this, that Unc, as Adrian called him, would be witty and waspish. I knew he would be honest and uncompromising. I knew he would make you snort, make you guffaw, make you wince, make you throw your hands up, make you think. But I had no idea where Adrian would go with him, or how far. Much farther than I could have imagined, at times much farther than I would have wished, and then farther still. In a little under six years he wrote close to sixty *Esquire* columns and, believe me, he had no intention of stopping. By the end they were mini surrealist masterpieces, gob-stoppingly weird. His final column – though none of us knew it would be, including him – purported to be a fantastically (or perhaps authentically) misogynist diatribe from Donald Trump. It was, as so often, a virtuoso display.

Adrian was tickled by *Esquire* readers' responses to the Unc columns. "It's the one thing that people come up to me in the street about," he once said. "They don't come up and talk to me about food and television, or African politics. But they will ask me about *Esquire*. The thing that everybody says is, 'Are the questions real?' And they are real. The fact they're written by me doesn't make them unreal. I always say, 'Yes, they are. Trust me: I'm Uncle Dysfunctional.'"

He was chuffed that we – me, the staff of the magazine, our readers – found the scatological gags and the flamboyant swearing funny. But Uncle Dysfunctional offered more than pungent puerility and phantasmagoric flights of fancy. There was profundity, too, and serious points were made – about sex and sexuality, men and women and other men and other women, parents and children, work and play, ethics and immorality. But, as you are about to discover, he never let more important concerns get in the way of a good knob joke.

I'm listed as the editor of these columns, and Adrian flattered me, from time to time, by describing me as that in conversation. But "editor" isn't quite right, not in my case anyway. "Stenographer" would have been more accurate. Or perhaps just "audience". That's not false modesty. I took dictation over the phone (all of these columns were filed direct to me or to my colleague, Rachel Fellows) and then, at best, helped shape the astonishing screed into traditional prose, with punctuation and paragraphs and the rest of it. Hardly ever did we change a word. Certainly we didn't rewrite him. There was no need. He spoke-wrote in perfect sentences, with the beats and the pauses all there. It took no great skill to see where one ought to place the commas and the full stops.

Adrian was collegiate, then. He often spoke of journalism as a team sport, and I am forever grateful to have had him on my team. But Uncle Dysfunctional was his alone. No one else could have done it, no one ever will.

I know he hoped these columns might make a book in the end (we talked about it more than once). All of us involved are thrilled that they have. We only wish he were here to see it published.

But enough of that. Time to pull up a chair and tell Adrian what the matter is. Girl trouble? Problem at work?

Losing your hair? Bent penis? Angry vagina? Not sure whether to bump off your better half? Recurring dreams of giving your boss a blowjob? Worried about the ethics of fantasising about your wife's younger sister? Irresistibly drawn to cravats/nudity? Wondering whether there's a god? Want the final, definitive, no-arguments ruling on whether size matters?

Whatever it is, it won't be something Uncle Dysfunctional hasn't heard before and ruled on, firmly and fiercely. And if he doesn't have the cure for what ails you, he'll certainly have something to say about it. Something silly, something sage. Something that'll put hairs on your chest, or make you want to cross your legs. On that, you can depend.

Alex Bilmes
London
February 2017

Sir,

I'm an American recently posted to England by my firm. Should I start saying sorry for things that are clearly not my fault, pretending to be more useless than I really am? I want to fit in.

Todd, London

Of course you should start fucking apologising. What is it you imagine isn't your fault? It's all your bleeding fault. If you didn't start it you made it worse. And if you didn't make it worse you didn't sort it out. You want to know why you need to start apologising? Look at your letter. How did you start that? "I'm an American." You could have said, "I'm a bald accountant." "I'm a great shag." "I'm a power-walker." "I'm someone who cries at films, but only on my own." There are an infinite number of ways we can identify ourselves, a whole wide emotional world of possible self-worth and introduction: father, son, husband, friend, colleague . . . But you chose "American". You want to wear the national superpower hero suit? This is the first and most important thing you can think of saying about yourself? Well, fine. Then you can take on all the responsibility and accountability for all the fuck-ups and dumb shit that goes with it. They couldn't get Hillary Clinton to do the job so

1

we got you. If you want to fit in and have a good time perhaps you might consider rephrasing that. "Hi, I'm a visitor." Or, "I'm new here." Have a nice day.

Dear Sir,
Is there any way to choose paint with your wife without it descending into a row?

Simon, Kensington

I don't have a wife. I don't know who it is you've been arguing with. I did have a wife. If you're rucking with her about paint, good luck mate. You're in for a world of beige. With taupe accents. And don't even start on tiles.

Mr Gill,
I've been pretending to like football for years because it seemed
the thing to do. Can I stop now?

Anon.

No. Not while you're still managing Chelsea.

Dear AA,

I haven't read a book since I left university in 1994. Am I missing out?

Alex, Northampton

I don't know. What else haven't you done since you left university? Had a whipped cream fight? Jumped off a bridge? Talked about French films for five hours? Slept with a friend and remained just friends? Been so happy to see your mates on a Friday night you thought you'd burst? Spent a whole term in a wife-beater trying to flick cards into a bin and smoke Gitanes at the same time? Woken up under a tree? Broken up over politics? You see, Alex, when people write about things they're not doing it's usually a symptom of a greater malaise, a deeper depression. If you want to know if you've missed out on reading books, go to a fucking bookshop and try a few. They won't mind, promise. If you left university in '94, my guess is you're just about hitting your 10,000-mile reality check. You're doing an inventory of what you've achieved. And comparing it with the to-do list you had when you turned 20. And it's a shock. There have been quite a lot of breakages. And pilfering. And it's way past its sell-by date. You either feel trapped or let down. And you realise it's not all still in front of you. It's not all

5

to play for. Half of it's already been used up. And you'll be lucky if you grab a draw. And the pattern for what the next 35 years is going to be like is already set. The horizon is closer, the panorama narrower, the goal smaller, the rewards prosaic. My guess is you didn't read a lot of books at university. And the degree you took was not much more than a label to get you three years of brilliant fun. And the further from it you get the more brilliantly it shines, and by contrast how much dimmer and more predictable your current life seems. But don't despair. There's an answer – it's not complicated. It's: suck in your gut and get on with it. This is the human condition. Live with it. In particular, it's the male human condition. When you were 20 you were a twat: insufferable, arrogant, thoughtless, boastful. You imagined all sorts of shit. You thought you'd be mates forever. You thought making money was about charm and being in the right place at the right time. You thought a plastic tube with a squeezy bulb would make your willy bigger and that being good in bed was a trick you did with your fingers, like shadow puppets. You thought England would win the World Cup before you were 30 and Salt-N-Pepa were the coolest hip-hop combo ever. So why should your post A-level wish list be any more reliable? The one thing you didn't have then was this paunch of self-pity. My advice is, whatever it is you think is holding you back or conspiring against you, embrace it. Do more of it. If it's responsibility you hate, take on more of it. If it's work, stay later. That's counterintuitive, but, trust me, without exception, the escape plans men make for themselves are all risible, pathetic, callow, selfish and destructive. Live with it.

This is what you're supposed to feel. This is being a man. Actually, on second thoughts, yes, you are missing out. Books, novels, are a great consolation. That's why they were invented, why they're written.

Mr Gill,

I've been told that flowers in pots aren't a socially acceptable gift, and that red roses are infra dig *and carnations are common. I don't understand any of this, because I am common. I was brought up in a tower block in Sheffield. My mum was a dinner lady, my dad worked for the gas board. Flowers were for weddings and funerals. I'm very, very successful and very, very smart. The people I have to work and mix with seem to know this stuff genetically. Can you give me a quick guide? I know it doesn't matter but it sort of does.*

Rick, London

I could tell you that the only acceptable roses are white or very faintly pink, but not salmon. And that long stems without thorns, in boxes, are laugh-out-loud embarrassing. And that all orchids are always hopelessly Thai Airways and that flowers mixed with vegetables are very passé and that tight balls of trimmed blooms in carefully complementary hues are so over. And never, ever send dried flowers or lilies with the stamens cut out or almost anything out of season. But contrarily, things that look like funeral decorations are bizarrely rather chic. And ideally cut flowers should look like they came from your garden and that your garden needs a tractor to drive round it and has a greenhouse the size of a tennis court. And never hand over flowers. They must be delivered, but not by a flower shop. They should come instantly after the event you're being grateful or apologising for. That is, within eight hours, including weekends and bank holidays. I could tell you all that. But I'm not going to. Put it out of your mind. Cast it into the Pit of Forgotten. Because you're right. We don't have to be told this. We do know it genetically. And you will always get something wrong. The wrong card. The wrong ink. The wrong words. The wrong sign-off. There is no end to this stuff. It's like nuclear physics. You think you've found the smallest possible particle of snobbery but there's always something more negligibly, minutely irrational. And you're also right to say it doesn't matter. What does matter is that you're not quite successful enough. Give it a couple of years, propelled by your obvious Lawrentian resentment, you'll do better than all of them. And then when all of your friends are posh employees, you can give them what you like. Paper flowers, bags of gypsophilia seeds. They will love and respect you from the bottom of their prune-like hearts. And I promise you still won't feel any less uncomfortable and they won't feel a scintilla less entitled.

Dear Sir,
Matching his and hers tattoos: ever acceptable?

Winston, Manchester

Only if you're Danish bacon.

AA,

My fiancé's from Glasgow. He's insisting on getting married in a kilt. I'm from Utah. My family are very conservative and religious. They're not going to understand. How can I get him into trousers without hurting his ethnic feelings?

Mary-Beth, by email

Ethnic feelings? He's from fucking Glasgow, for Christ's sake. The kilt is the least of your worries. Even when they find out what he's not got on underneath, and they surely will, wait till your parents get a load of the in-laws and his childhood mates. The reception is going to be fabulous. Are you writing this up as a film treatment? If not, do you mind if I have it? PS, do you seat your mothers by height or age?

11

Dear Sir,
When, if ever, is it permissible for a man to sign off a text with "love" or "x"? And don't say "best" is best, because it isn't. Nor "yours" nor "faithfully" nor "peace".

Love Derek x

Darling, sweetheart, cupcake. It's permissible, as you sweetly put it, to sign texts any damn way you like. You're all so bloody fond of the internet and you bang on and on about messaging and techno and plugged-in stuff, and you say it's all about freedom and honesty, and the day after you get a Twitter account you're all constipated about the raised-pinkie etiquette of how to say "cheerio", and all the rest of the manners business and the after-you niceties. You sound like my grandparents. Why do you care? Why do you want to start making up rules and laws and a smirking snobbery about something you say is pristine, anarchic and lawless, and naked? If it's any help, Alexander Graham Bell suggested that you answered his implement with a firm and clear, "Ahoy". So why not start with that? And why don't you finish with . . .

❖   ❖   ❖

Dear AA Gill,

My wife and I went on holiday with her family. Her younger sister came down to the pool wearing a tiny bikini. "Ooh," I said, "that's one for the wank bank." I wasn't really sure if I said it out loud. The wife went tonto. "Did you just say you wanted to masturbate over my sister?" I tried to explain the harmless concept of the wank bank, that all men have one. But she won't let it go. She has to know who else is in it, and if she's there. And every time we go to a restaurant or a pub she says, "I suppose she's a deposit in your savings account." And now she's asking her friends if their husbands have them, and the guys are complaining to me. But the worst bit is, I'm experiencing difficulties taking Captain Picard to warp speed. Where there should be Angelina Jolie in leather or Halle Berry in sweat, I can only see the wife, wagging her finger and shouting, "I hope that's not my sister in there with you!"

Phil, by email

There is a wank-banking crisis. We all speculated and spent, in the biblical sense – borrowed from one ball to pay to the other – on fantasies of body parts we can't sustain, or pay the interest. The 21st-century wank bank is full of arses and tits we don't need, and we'll never use. It looks like your iTunes library but without the sense of rhythm or a

Genius button. And does it make us happy, all this ejaculatory aspiration? No, it doesn't. Tell the wife she's right. In these straitened times you can't afford a big, fuck-off-I'm-busy wank bank. So you're laying them all off except for a couple of tasteful classical statues and that memory of her with the sunburn and the drunken Brazilian on honeymoon, and that from now on you're placing yourself in her hands or outsourcing to the internet.

Mr Gill,
I'm frightened.

Anonymous, by email

And so you should be. Frightened is the natural state for all men. There is much to be frightened about and of. What's more frightening is you don't know the half of it. The measure of a man's life is how he copes with the terrible wall of fear. The traditional manly remedies are: rigorous self-delusion (an absolute refusal to face anything remotely akin to reality or even open an envelope); drink; and mood-altering masturbation. And for this you need a really comprehensive wank bank.

Sir,

My husband said he had something important to tell me. I could see from the fear it was serious. I'd suspected for some time that he might have been wearing my clothes, so I was prepared for a bout of tearful trannie guilt. Which, frankly, I'd be OK with. We're about the same size and I didn't marry him for his dress sense, so I might as well stay married to him for mine. But then he blurted out that he was a nudist. I must say I was surprised. Calmly, I said I thought I might have noticed if he'd been playing volleyball in the garden starkers. He said he didn't want to be a collective nudist – he was a singular, secret one. And he would like me to be a secret nudist with him. What, just round the house? No, he said. Outside, together. Well I wasn't overcome with excitement, but compromise is everything in a relationship, and after 20 years of marriage I was amazed that there was anything new to discover about him. I'm going to draw a veil over our sojourn in Hampstead Heath. If only I'd had a veil about me at the time. Never again. He said the deeply humiliating cascade of events was my fault for not being quick enough. He is still sulking. And he says he doesn't know if we can go on if I can't join him on his journey. At the moment I don't know if I can go on if I do. It does seem a very stupid reason to break up what is essentially a happy though dull life with a nice home, a successful business and a secure family.

Sophie, West Sussex

He is not a nudist. Nudists are plural. A singular nudist is a flasher. He wants to implicate you in his sad little waggling insecurity. If he gets nicked on his own it's six months on the nonce's wing and a lifetime on the register. If he's got you with him it's a Benny Hill sketch, and the bobbies trying to keep a straight face while giving you a lift home in a blanket, with a verbal to lay off the Viagra and go on holiday to Sweden. But you're right not to want to break up a perfectly dull marriage. It's not that serious. It's not as if he suggested bridge, or restoring classic caravans. The answer is, introduce him to your nearest art school as a model. He can be naked alone and observed. And you could take up sketching, and thus join in while remaining clothed. Indeed, you sound like someone who might take to bohemian headscarves, smocks, lumpy jewellery and cannabis. And you can't be any worse at art than he is at being a pervert.

Dear Mr Gill,

My husband has a degenerative, incurable illness. We're both young, under 30. We met at school and have been together since GCSE geography. Now he wants to die and he wants me to help him and assumes I will because we love each other. He says I won't get into trouble with the police, and courts are sympathetic to spouses who assist in suicides – particularly after Terry Pratchett – and anyway I have no ulterior motive. He's saying goodbye to all his friends and making arrangements for the big day: drugs, suffocation and Billie Holiday. He's happier than he's been for ages. The thing is, I do have an ulterior motive. I'm sleeping with his younger brother. And have been for years. In fact, I was on the point of leaving when he got diagnosed, but then I couldn't. I've just discovered I'm pregnant and obviously it can't be my husband's. Oh, and there's one other thing. It doesn't really matter but my husband's father has a title. If he dies it will pass to his brother. And he'll inherit a great deal of land. I do think killing him is the best option. I have no problems either way, morally.

Jocasta, London SW3

Congratulations. Hats off. Respect. You can be in this business for years without getting a problem that impressively screwed up. Where did you all go to school? Webster's

Academy of Jacobean Tragedy? OK, here's the thing: you're completely fucked. No, really. Game over. There is just one teeny, forlorn chink of hope, an outside, 100–1 chance. So here is your mission, if you choose to accept it. First you've got to tell the husband that he's going to be a father. Explain the immaculate conception by telling him you judiciously had some of the hereditary custard frozen, way back, just in case. And you've secretly been having IVF. You didn't tell him because you didn't want him to be disappointed if it didn't work. So he has to stay alive to see his son. You have to square the brother, carrot and stick. First, keep shagging him, which shouldn't be a hardship. But tell him if he says anything you'll deny it and no one will believe him because he's a younger son, and no one ever believes younger sons. So this way you keep everything, including someone else's good name. But, and there is a but, the child will grow to be an amoral, manipulative, sensual monster. The two of you will be well-suited until you get old and the last thing you'll see is his beautiful smile as he gently but firmly holds a pillow embroidered with the family crest over your face.

Sir,
I've just left uni and have got a lot of job interviews lined up.
City, industry, etc. I'm really clever. My CV's impressive. I'm
sure I could do most jobs better than most people but I'm shit at
interviews. When someone asks me what my chief fault is, I have
an uncontrollable desire to say, "I smile when listening to idiots."
And then smile.

Gareth, via Facebook

OK, Gareth. First, remember this is all about the job. It's not just about *your* job. It's all to do with the jobs of the people who are interviewing you. Being on a recruitment panel represents a lot of stress and an opportunity for people in offices. They get to show off or get shown up. There will be one boss-person and then two underling suits, who will be trying to outdo each other. What they're looking for is someone who makes them look good, and who won't be a threat. So the trick to interviews is not the dos, but the three don'ts. Don't flirt, don't be too keen and don't be too clever. Remember, the job will always go to the third best candidate. First and second best will be championed by the competing courtiers. The boss will say, "Is there anyone we can all agree on?" And that'll be third best. Which is never going to be you, is it? Because the other thing is, you're a twat. A proper, whiny, pompous, self-justifying twat. I hope *The Big Issue* thing works out for you.

AA,

My girlfriend's just been diagnosed with bipolar disorder. It's such a downer. Can I dump her?

Chinua, by email

Yeah, course you can. Hey, you didn't sign up for a mentalist, did you? Don't feel bad. No reason why you both should. She'll probably be better off on her own. She can concentrate on lightening the fuck up. I wouldn't risk a face-to-face. Might make her worse: the begging, the what-did-I-do-wrong sobbing, the suicide threats. Just text her. "Sorry, babe, not working out for me. Moving on. Cheer up. LOL."

Dear Uncle Dysfunctional,
It's our one-month anniversary and I'm taking my girlfriend to
Paris for the weekend. I want to give her some nice underwear
for the occasion. I don't know where to start.

Tom, Putney

Jesus. She's already wearing your bollocks as earrings. No
man in the history of shagging has ever remembered or
acknowledged a one-month anniversary. Look, Tom, these
are the rules for lingerie: don't. Simple as. Your job is getting
it off, not adding to it. That's all you've got to remember.
Never, ever, give underwear. You don't know her size. Her
friends will lie about her size. She'll lie about her size. Take
an old bra into Agent Provocateur and the shop assistant
will lie about her size. Just going, "Oh, about a handful",
isn't enough. Men and women see completely different
things when they look at bras and knickers. No woman who
doesn't keep tenners in her garter belt has ever worn red
underwear. Men put on their Berlusconi heads when they
step through the door of Victoria's Secret. Women grow
instantly frigid when presented with a bra and thong set.
What they see is a whole night of humiliation and logistical
and ergonomic problems. Any man who could choose
aesthetic, sensual underwear in the correct size is not the

sort of man they'd want to wear it for. Here's what you need to know about erotic presents and Paris: give her a riding crop. Unless she's got a horse. If she's already got a horse it's not an erotic present, it's a cheap gift.

Dear Adrian,

I'm just starting at a Southern uni. No one from my family, school or estate in the North East has ever been to university. I can handle the work. I get on with the other students. I'm not teased or bullied. I'm popular and everyone likes my accent. It's all cool except I really can't handle the dressing up. Why are middle-class, privately educated Southern kids so childishly obsessed with fancy dress? Every Friday night the town and campus looks like a cross between a hen night and MGM's backlot. The streets are littered with vomiting bunnies and discarded togas. Every event comes with some embarrassing instruction to dress up as your favourite sin or an animal with the first letter of your name. Or there are instructions on what to arrive as, and then find your blind date who'll be dressed as Wilma to your Fred, or Courtney to your Kurt. I've just had another one from my tutor that says, "Dress: smart-casual". What the fuck is "smart-casual"? Come as an oxymoron?

Clive, by email

Clive, you've stepped into the pantyhose of class, the last codpiece of the English class system. Everything else – the Empire, the deference, the big house, the cosy snobbery and a gardener with only one name – has been taken away from them. All that's left are tarts and vicars parties. And if you want to feel really out of place, turn up as a vicar. All posh English boys want to dress up as women. They can't see a balloon without sticking it up their jumpers. If you want to separate the public schoolboys from the comprehensive ones, just put them in a room with a wig. The reasons for this are many, deep and distressing. Don't go there. On a fundamental level, the class system was always about fancy dress. A hierarchy of funny hats, ribbons, chains, breeches, riding, shooting, Henley and judges. It's been pointed out (by badly dressed Americans) that the English ruling class has clothes instead of character. Their whole lives are spent dressing up to be someone else. When they say clothes maketh the man, they mean it literally. They have kit to be brave in, kit to be clever in, kit to be romantic in and pyjamas with flies that don't work for rudimentary sex. Your best bet is to play to the stereotype. Have a couple of default costumes: a Jarrow marcher; a coal miner; or Rodney Bewes from *The Likely Lads*. As for smart-casual, no one knows what it means. It's the garment version of "How are you?" or "I'll give you a ring." An empty instruction, a request without emphasis or meaning. It's just there to stop people phoning up all week asking, "How should I dress for your drinks party?" It means, not a dressing gown or the robes for the Order of the Garter. And in your case, I think the Rodney Bewes outfit will be fine.

AA,
I have a large penis. We're not talking above average. I mean
huge. Thick and long. And white. A really, really big white penis.
Anonymous, by email

On your shoulders?

Hi,

My name's Gerald. I've been in analysis for seven years, but my shrink's away on her summer holidays and I really need someone to talk to. You look a bit like her and you also look a bit like my dad. I've had a sort of OK week. I think I'm dealing with the passive-aggressive stuff, though I did have this moment, an encounter – not so much an encounter, just like a passing thing, not important really – with this woman in a car park at Tesco. She was old, well not old, older than me. But nice-looking in a sort of seen-better-days way. I helped her load the shopping into the back of her car. It was a VW. I still get these pangs of irrational fear around German cars. Then she offered me a probiotic yoghurt as a thank-you. Fucking hell! What's that all about? I was filled with rage. What did she mean? I mean really mean? Did she see me as a child, a helpful boy with undescended testicles, not a real man? Do I need my bowels opened? It brought up issues about penis length, cleanliness and my terror of sphincters. I mean, she could have given me a banana. She had a bunch. So there was that, which I think I dealt with quite well. The yoghurt gave me wind. The bitch next door, with the cat, the one whose bedroom I can see into and had the minor obsession with, well, it's been pissing in my garden. The cat, not Laura. I actually caught it spraying the Japanese Maple where I put my dad's ashes and the posthumous letter I wrote him. This seems over-

loaded with significance. Bitch. Pussy. Dad. Writing. Canadian national symbol . . . [The rest of this letter can be read on help-myanalystisonholidayandihavenoonetotalkto.com*]*

The thing with analysis, Gerald – I'm assuming Gerald isn't your real name; Gerald hasn't been anyone's real name since the war – is that analysis is a good thing. Self-knowledge is a good thing. A karmic manicure is a good thing. Here's the other thing: people who need analysis but haven't had any can be really fun to be around, because they're nuts. People who have had analysis can be really fun to be around because they're not nuts. It's the people *in* analysis that are fucking insufferable. They have half the understanding, which is like knowing half the rules of chess. You're no fun to play with. So while you're in analysis, that's a decade when no one's going to want to know you, particularly your mother. And by the way, she's not on holiday, she's moved.

Uncle D,
What's your position on pornography?

Ava, by email

Complaining about pornography is like moaning about the weather, though more fun, with better graphics. We are just surrounded by it. It's bottomless, topless and endless. It's also very repetitive. Very, very, very repetitive. So I don't have a position on porn. I'm assuming this is a sniggering pun and you're not called Ava. You're probably Gerald. And you're 14 and your penis looks like the handlebar grips on a midwife's Riley. What the nuanced social observer, the postmodern moral philosopher has in place of a position is more a voyeuristic, hand on chin, quizzically smiling anthropological interest in particular sorts of pornography. If you are in doubt of what that is, there is a helpful index to the left-hand side of most porn sites. You can choose which ones to take umbrage at. Racial stereotypes for instance. Black men, big cocks. Japanese girls, white socks. Fake lesbian exploitation. Unshaven German creampie Milf compilation. Porn is no longer either/or. It's sometimes and somethings. But don't let anyone tell you that what you need is to be more open to porn, Gerald. Don't ever get lulled into sharing it or watching it with your girlfriend (when you get one) as some sort of foreplay. This is disgusting and unnatural. Porn has to be solitary, singular, secret and, above all, embarrassing. Nothing ruins pornography like someone else cranking one out saying, "Can't we fast forward through this bit? Oh, and the midget's got a willy just like yours."

Mr Gill,

I've got this boyfriend, and on the face of it he ticks every box, some of them more than once. He's good-looking, solvent, with an indoor, sitting-down job. He's got a car that's insured, which is as rare as morris dancers round here. My family love him, and so do I. It's all lush, until he opens his bleeding mouth. He's got this accent. He sounds posh. Like off Downton Abbey, *or some black and white film. Normally I can handle it because he's polite and funny. It's just in bed, his voice does me in. You really can't talk dirty and sound sexy with a posh accent. It's like being rogered by a comedy butler or a magistrate. I can't take it seriously. Every time he says, "Here I come ready or not." Or, "Good Lord, brill top bollocks, Miss." Or, "Steady the bus!" (he says that quite a lot), I go off the whole thing. I'm writing to you because I assume you're posh. How do any of you actually breed? How can you get a throb-on for some bird who sounds like Princess Anne saying stuff like, "Do you have a reservation?"*

Cher, by instant message

Ah, Tracy. Do you mind if I call you Tracy? I know it's not your name, but you're all Tracys to us. Of course, you're completely right. Received pronunciation, BBC English, or "posh", is good for many things: ordering thousands of oiks to almost certain death; governing an empire with not much more than five drunken Scotsmen and a cricket bat. It's brilliant for memorial services, patronising foreigners, children and horses and, bizarrely, poetry. But God in His wisdom gives and He takes away. Even though He obviously has the same accent as your boyfriend, He has deemed it the most preposterous voice when naked. When all is said and done, or done then said, it is the accent of understatement. And if engaged in the beast with 20 toes and a single desire, you really don't want understatement, or to sound phlegmatically sophisticated. No one wants to hear, "Whenever you're ready old girl" as a soundtrack to the vinegar strokes. My suggestion is to shove a pillow in his mouth. It will remind him of school. Or wear earphones playing *Get Carter*. Of course, if you're serious about the chap then work up some ruse to get him fired, get one of your mates to nick his car and insist he moves in with you. In a couple of months he'll sound like your bruvas. We are not born with this accent. We achieve it. It's part of our training. Take away the perks and the position and we lose the accent. Anyway, in our heads we all sound just like you. Out loud we may be saying, "I say! Tally-ho!" In our heads it sounds like, "Eat cock snot, bitch."

Dear Uncle Dysfunctional,
I'm short.

Leon, by email

Lie down.

Dear AA,

I had one girlfriend at uni. We were each other's first loves, and inseparable. It was really intense. We went on to live together for a year. I thought we'd probably start a family, but out of the blue (or so it seemed to me) she left me for another woman, saying she'd always sort of known she was gay. I was utterly gutted and de-nutted and I had a bad couple of years. But I met someone else and we married and have a nice life together. I never completely lost touch with my old girlfriend; we've remained friends, though not close. She and her partner (the same one) want to start a family, and she's asked me to be the donor. I can't say I wasn't surprised, but I've thought about it and I think I should: they're in a stable relationship, there wouldn't be any financial commitment from me and it would be a way of saying there's no hard feelings and I'd like to help. My problem is: how do I tell my wife? We don't have any children.

Ahmed, Bushey

No hard feelings, Ahmed? No hard feelings? This whole letter is written in the pale ink of hard feelings, on thin-skinned notepaper. The envelope is stuck down with bitter bile. It's stamped with regret. To say there are no hard feelings, only shows that you have the sensitivity of an angle grinder. OK, you're not over it. No one ever gets over being dumped. You learn to live with it. You grow a scab and then a tough lump that you stroke occasionally. You spend a couple of hundred words talking about your ex, you mention the wife in passing and the fact that she's childless as a postscript. I'm assuming you haven't bred because there's a blockage. And it's hers not yours. I'm assuming the honest reason you want to donate your tadpoles to the dyke bitch who broke your Bambi heart is because you want the revenge hump, even if it's just with a syringe. So, leaving aside the obvious answer – which is "No!! Not conceivably, you dense fuckwit!!" – these are the options. One: don't say anything to the wife, slip the ex her shot of man fat purchased from a stranger found in the waiting room of your local STD clinic, preferably a bloke who's chromatically very different from you. This is the revenge option. It will give you an instant, huge sense of release, a lightness of being. You will feel like you have been given an extra lung and the steel band has been removed from around your head. It will last for half an hour. And then you will feel sad and guilty for the rest of your life. But guilty sadness might be easier than the fawning anger you're weighed down with at the moment. Then there is the option of Solomon: you say yes to the ex but with conditions. You give her two shots, one for her, one for her partner. It's a twofer deal. They both get pregnant. They keep one child. You and your wife adopt the other.

Fun fact: there's a lot of inventive thinking going on about human insemination at the moment. What you might call in-the-box thinking. One entrepreneur is opening an online sperm boutique. He's looking to make attractive cocktails of shot juice for ladies who want children but not the whingeing demands of exhausting infants – so, no fathers. He's putting together collegiate shots, collections of mixed jiz with a common theme. So you might get a football team's spunk, the whole of Man U in an Actimel bottle, or, if you're on a budget, Norwich. You could have the cast of *West Side Story*. Or, when the sprog asks who its dad is, you could say the faculty of the London School of Economics, or the Household Cavalry Sovereign's Escort. He's thinking of taking commissions for bespoke screws. The oddest request was from a professional Swedish lady who's after the collective DNA of London's zookeepers.

Dear Uncle Dysfunctional,
I've got a bent cock. Really bent. Like a right angle. What shall I do?

Rupert, Oxford

Go fuck yourself.

Dear Adrian,

I love my wife. We've been married 10 years, got two great kids, she's a brilliant mum, makes our house a wonderful home, is funny, popular, and supportive. We share lots of interests. I can't imagine my life without her. But she's a minger. I don't fancy her. Not at all. I'm not sure I ever did; you know, we were young, I was drunk. She's an awkward shape and ugly – but only on the outside. It's a terrible thing. I really can't shag her. So I've been pretending I've got erectile dysfunction. Don't laugh. Of course she's really understanding and tells me not to worry. But most of the time I'm bent over with an angry diamond cutter. I'm horribly horny and wanking like a choirboy. This has gone on for a year now. But I think it's coming to a head, and not in a good way. I've seen on the family computer that she's ordered a load of Viagra. It's my birthday in a month and I'm sure this is going to be my treat, along with the Victoria's Secret thong, the chocolate lube and the Leona Lewis CD. What am I going to do? I'm desperate. Please don't suggest makeovers, or surgery or party frocks. It would just make her look even more like Grayson Perry. I know this all sounds funny but I'm really sad. I love my wife with all my heart, and I could never ever countenance an affair.

Graham, by email

Graham, you've learnt a very useful and character-building lesson. All men occasionally wonder what it would be like to be a woman. Well, now you know. What you so touchingly describe is exactly how most married women feel about their husbands, though without the good-with-kids-good-around-the-house supportive bit. All women sooner or later end up married to an unshaggable bloke, and you don't even pretend to make an effort. When was the last time you bought a new pair of pants? You think only Italians and ladyboys clip their nose hair. Take off your clothes, Graham. Get naked. Look in the mirror. See what your wife sees. Now get a stiffy. Most people marry into their league. Pretty people marry other pretty people. Munter meets munter. It's your genes – they're looking for a good fit. They want staying power, not a transient surprise result. Five doesn't go into 10. The only couples who move from the Endsleigh League into the Championship are the very rich or deranged. So if your wife is an awkward shape, and ugly, chances are, so are you. But being a man you'll imagine this doesn't matter. Well, wake up and smell the bellend, Graham. You have choices. The Mr Rochester: a bit drastic, having to blind yourself. Try turning the lights out. Or just man up. Take a blue pill, do the business and be grateful. And when it comes round to her birthday, tell her you've got a surprise. Get her really drunk, slip her a roofie and have the naked bird of your fantasy choice tattooed on her back. When she comes round, tell her that you'd suggested a dolphin on her ankle but she insisted. It's not ideal, but it should see you through till the annoying urges go away.

Uncle,

I'm going to spend the night with my first girlfriend. She's given me a written list of what we're going to do: takeaway pizza, bottle of cider, The X Factor, *petting on the sofa, and up to bed for sex. She says she expects full reciprocal oral sex. I've been researching it on the internet, but I'm confused. It looks horrible. Can you help?*

Oliver, by email

OK, get a pomegranate. Cut a v-shaped slice out of it. Put your hands behind your back and eat the seeds without using your teeth. For the full Sensurround effect, push a teaspoon of warm lard up each nostril.

Dear Uncle,

I'm 17 and beginning to show signs of male-pattern baldness. My mates call me Wills. I laugh it off and pretend I don't care, but I do. It's so unfair. It saps my confidence. I laugh at men with comb-overs, but I'm beginning to brush my hair forward and wear little hats. Please, please tell me something useful, and don't mention Yul Brynner. My stepmum and all her friends always say, "Look at Yul Brynner!" I've no idea who he is.

Francis, by email

Yul Brynner, 1920–1985. Film actor who pretended to be a Mongol. Was in fact a Swiss-Russian gypsy, most famous for being bald. He is a terrible eggsample of a man whose life was defined by what he wasn't: hairy. Baldness is a bugger, because it's obvious and it's obviously not that serious. It's not going to kill you. It's only follicle-deep. Loads of people are bald, and it's what's in your head that's more important than what's on it, etc., etc. But we all know it is important. I've just asked five girls under 30 if they minded bald men. Four of them said it was a deal-breaker. The fifth said she didn't mind, but between you and me she's a bit of a spoon-faced dog. So there you have it. Best to learn this lesson early. Everyone in the world would rather have lots of hair on themselves and their partners than none at all. And you'll get no sympathy. Being bald isn't like being ethnic or disabled. Everyone can and will make jokes about it and expect you to laugh good-naturedly, which you will. You will also buy all the lotions, drops, creams and patent cures that you know are humiliating rip-offs. You will spend years looking in mirrors, flicking your fingers through your spindly temples. You will try a ponytail on holiday. And finally you will have implants that look like a dollhouse's Italian garden. You'll marry a girl who pretends not to mind your pate because you pretend not to mind her facial warts. Toughen up. There's still 40 years to go before the inescapable slip into Bruce Forsyth's syrup. Oh, the other thing that Yul Brynner was famous for was having a humongous cock. His head looked like his bell-end, only smaller. I'm guessing this isn't your compensation.

Mr Gill,

*I'm marrying my long-term girlfriend next summer and already
there's a major family row. Sara comes from a Pakistani family.
While she's pretty much agnostic (no veil, bit of drink and blow,
lots of sex, no pork), her family are quite old-fashioned and
observant. They've always been very hospitable to me. I get on
with her brothers, and her mum's really nice because I don't see
mine much. In the house they're traditional, which I like. I'm
Irish. My parents are divorced. My mum lives in Australia. The
thing is my dad is a transvestite called Petra. Sara and she get
on really well. They talk about shoes and make-up, they go out
for drinks and to see her Shirley Bassey karaoke. Sara's family
wants to have a dinner at their house for my family. It's important to them. The thing is, men and women eat separately. They
all know about my dad and say he's welcome. She says she
shouldn't be welcome, she should sit in the room with the women
and children, and that not being treated as a second-class
woman is an infringement of her human rights, and discrimination. And anyway, she says, she's already bought a burka.
Sara says she's got a point and if it's that important to Dad,
then her family should just accept it as being part of living in a
Western godless society. On the other hand I think that Dad
should stop being such a big girl's blouse about it, man up and
put on a suit for the evening, if only for my sake. Sara and I are*

having a running row. When I try to point out the irony of an
Irish lapsed Catholic bloke defending a Muslim man, and a
Pakistani lapsed Muslim sticking up for an old Paddy hod-car-
rier in a sparkly frock, she says this is serious, because it's a test
of my behaviour and fundamental understanding of women.
What if our son wants to dress up as Britney Spears, like his
granddad? Sort this out.

Dermot, London

First, good question. OK, here's the answer. Tell your dad
that of course she must come as Petra, but what they'd
really like is if she could do her act, so why doesn't she take
a course in belly dancing and come and do the Dance of
the Seven Veils for the men? They'll love it (who wouldn't?),
Sara is placated because you're encouraging your father's
transgender self-determination, her family will think that
your lot are as mad as the Middle East with heatstroke –
but then they think that anyway – and they'll be touched
at the cultural effort that Petra's made. And of course you'll
probably be mortified with embarrassment, but then you're
used to that, aren't you? And like you said, it's only for one
night. So that's sorted. But Sara does have a point. What
would you do if your son wanted to dress up like Alice in
Alice in Wonderland? I sense that you're not quite as culturally
cool as you'd like us to think. You're happiest when everyone
agrees not to believe anything very much or very strongly.
It's nice when everything is relative and polite and dispos-
able. I expect the thing you like most about Sara's family
is that they have a strong set of values. Make a list of
everyone you wouldn't sit down at dinner with out of prin-

45

ciple. If it's shorter than the list of your friends or if there's no one on it at all, you need to do a lot of thinking, a lot of manning up, a lot of big-girl's-blouse work before you get married.

Sir,

My girlfriend has a really angry vagina. The rest of her is kind and gentle and really into me. From the waist up she couldn't be more loving. But her front bottom hates me. Sometimes I catch it scowling, giving me the evils. Have you noticed they follow you round the room with a death stare? I've mentioned it to the girlfriend. She just laughs and says why don't we kiss and make up? I did but it just lay there without even making an effort. And then it whispered to me that I was a twat-hating prick and it was going to suffocate me in the night. So I said, "Did you hear that?" And the girlfriend just gave me a weird smile and said I was so funny. So now I've noticed things are going missing. A cuff link. Some malaria pills. A chess set. And I know it's that lippy minge.

Steve, by email

You're right. So few men really look at vaginas. They've all got their own personalities. The good, the bad and the ugly. You need to be very careful. Never turn your back on a psycho clunge. When good beaver goes bad it's usually because they've been abused in the past, let down, laughed at. Lots of vaginas just nag. What time do you call this? You're drunk again. What do you think I am, a hotel? Clean up after yourself! You need to show the little lady hole you can be trusted. You're not like all the others.

Dear Mr Gill,

I don't read your magazine. I'm writing to you because I found it in my son's room. And I thought, rather desperately, that you might have some insight into the state of mind of your customers. Frankly I'm at the end of my tether. My boy Percival is a complete stranger to me. He doesn't appear to share a single one of my or his mother's values. It is as if our whole lives were a weathervane for him to set his face against. I feel like the anti-life. I can't understand how we can have had him in our care for 16 years yet so completely failed to inculcate a single civilised cultural or humane value in him. Percival regards us with an unveiled contempt. Barely utters a polite sentence. He would rather sit alone in the rain than share a meal with his mother and me. I sound angry, and I suppose I am. But really, I'm sad. He was such a beautiful little boy, such a joy for both of us. I had so many hopes and dreams for him. We were going to accomplish so much together. I miss him.

William, Gloucestershire

William. Come closer. Closer! Put your ear to the page. Hear that? That's the *Esquire* pity orchestra playing 100 sobbing violins. You bring up children and everything is for them: the house, the holidays. You put in the time and the money, you worry and you work, you stand on the touchline and you keep your fingers crossed, all for them. And then suddenly they hit puberty and it's all about you. Oh, the lack of gratitude, the undeserved contempt, the smelly ugliness of it all. It's as if you'd lovingly spent a decade and a half building an Airfix model of yourself only to find the picture on the box was a lie. Really, it was Sid Vicious. The point here is he's right and you're wrong. When he shouts that he didn't ask to be born, and you shout back that he didn't ask to finish the milk or take the car or throw a party or call his mother a cunt either, then he's right and you're petty. What you really mind and fear is that he's passing you by. Everything you think and stand for and believe will fade away. Everything he thinks and believes and stands for will grow brighter and louder until it takes over your world. What you choose to do now is going to set the tone and the consequences of the rest of his life. You can go on like you are and he may turn up for the odd Christmas and your funeral. Or you can seriously and humbly try to find out what it is he wants. What he aspires to. What he hopes for. And if you can do that without sneering or knowing better or saying, "That's not music. Whatever happened to melody?" Or, "Why don't any of you pull your trousers up?" Or, "If she were my daughter, I'd die of shame," then you could still do stuff together. Share things. But they need to be his things. His dreams, not yours. Yours are fading to black. You remember a beautiful boy. He remembers a smiling, proud dad. Who kicked a ball. And was pleased to see him. And didn't say, "Don't talk like that in front of your mother." The Librarian of Hull said that parents fuck you up. Of course, being childless himself he didn't go on to point out that it was nothing like as much as kids fuck up their parents.

Dear Uncle Dysfunctional,
I've got an itchy arse. Really itchy. Sometimes it's like an ant's
Olympics up there. Should I do something about it?

Julian, New York

You bet. Get an aardvark digit up there and do the starfish samba. Surf that itch. Here's the thing with the arse itch. It can have any number of causes. But they're unimportant. What matters is that the itch that dare not speak its name is one of the greatest pleasures in life. An effervescent ring is the fundamental joy of being a man. It is the back door to endorphins, a secret cave of shuddering relief. Few simple pleasures are as blissfully rewarding as getting down and dirty with the little boy's itch. Followed by that intense guilty stab of pain. And then the long moments of reverie, secretly smelling your fingernail. That's the good stuff, man. You get your haemorrhoids frozen, or the dhobi itch cortizoned, what are you left with? A sewage outlet. Where's the fun in that? The Emma Freuds are one of the few diseases where the cure is worse than the condition.

❖   ❖   ❖

Mr AA,

I keep having this weird dream that I'm giving my boss a blowjob. It's really graphic. I wake up with a massive hard-on. In real life we get on fine. I admire him. We play squash in our lunch hour. But nothing pervy. Do you think that I'm subconsciously gay, or just ambitious? Should I be worried?

Geoff, Manchester

I don't know, Geoff. Should you be? If your boss were a woman and you had a dream about going down on her, would it be a problem? Would you still be ambitious? Would you have written a letter asking if you should be worried? Why is the possibility you might be gay any more disturbing than the possibility you might be straight? When you bought this magazine, did your hand just slip off *Vogue?* The simplest way to find out if you're gay is to get stuck in. Have a go. Ask your boss if he fancies a gobble after squash. And if you do it more than twice, chances are you're both gay. Congratulations. Life's looking up. You just got regular sex, a better wardrobe, and probably the key to the executive washroom.

❖　　❖　　❖

Sir,
What's with guy nipples? Like, what's the point?

Yusuf, by email

Well, there are two answers to this. One is the boring biological one and the other is the fun pick-up line. Lessons first: the scientific explanation is that while the sperm chooses the sex of a foetus, in the dark we are all omnisexual. It could go either way. When the male sex organs are being made it would be too much trouble to remove the nipples, which are probably modified sweat glands, so they're left on as ornaments. Females get on and construct a mammary system, and you both get to enjoy the Victoria's Secret website. Almost all male mammals have nipples. But I seem to remember that mice don't. And I'm not sure about muntjac. That's the explanation. But it isn't wholly satisfying. Nature rarely leaves spare parts around. Natural selection doesn't like waste, or useless hangers on. Nothing is a design flaw. Particularly when nipples in humans are also a secondary sexual characteristic (though not in mice). But here's the thing. Although male nipples are sensitive and have an erectile capacity, I know of no straight men who like their nipples tinkered with. I've asked around, and most blokes actively hate it. The best I got was a shrugged

54

indifference from Giles Coren, metrosexual lothario and epicurean, who said, "Er, not especially. Bitten gently is nice but only if I'm already up and running. Not as a girl's first move." But I've also asked a handful of gay blokes, and, to a man, they say that the male nipple is a sensitive and important part of foreplay. Now this isn't a scientific study – well it's as scientific as most cosmetics studies – but we may be onto something. The point of the male nipple just might be the elusive gay button. If you're worried that you're a gayer or indeed vanilla straight, put Maria Callas on the iPod, take off your Ben Sherman, stand in front of a mirror, think of Ryan Gosling and gently run your thumb anti-clockwise over your nipples. Getting anywhere?

Dear Uncle,
Is there a god?

Celestine, London

Uh-uh. Wrong question. You meant to ask, should I care if there's a god? If the answer is yes, I do care, then yes, there is a god. If the answer is no, I don't care, then who cares? You see, it's not "does God exist", but "does faith exist"? People who know there is a god and people who know there isn't live in exactly the same world. Same number of hours in the day, same weather, same football results. They both love their children and die of the same diseases. People who don't believe in God are no happier than people who do, and those who don't believe are no nicer than those who don't. The answer is that if God exists, he doesn't seem to mind if you believe in him or not. The real question is: if you knew there was a god, would you behave any differently? And if the answer is yes, then perhaps you should assume there is.

Mate,
Is there a female G-spot?

Max, Edinburgh

See previous letter.

Dear Uncle Dysfunctional,

I've just been dumped. Oh, God, I can barely write it. I love him. I've loved him since the first moment I saw him in cricket whites at school. (I joined the sixth form of a boys' public school.) We started going out. We were each other's first lovers, in a sleeping bag in the New Forest. We read Auden together for the first time, climbed Ben Nevis together, shared jumpers and scrambled egg on toast with Marmite. We've been inseparable. I don't think I've done something until I've done it with him. No one knows me, will ever know me, like he does. I knew, I know, we are a perfect fit. We went to separate unis. I wasn't concerned because our love was so strong and beautiful. I never suspected, even when he cancelled a weekend together, but the next Monday I got a rambling email saying we'd got too entangled in each other's lives, we both needed space to make new friends, do new things. He said he would always love me and it would be a perfect memory and that in the future we'd be great friends, and there was no one else. Of course there's someone else; I know him so well. This is the worst thing that's ever happened. I had no idea you could feel this desperately sad. I'm frightened by the utter hopelessness of my misery. I can't stay at college. I can't go home. I can't bear to talk to other people. I can't bear to be on my own. I can't sleep. I can't be awake. I can't read, watch TV, listen to music, eat. I can't think of anything else. I can't be without him.

There is no hope. I would do anything, suffer anything, to be with him. His name is Luke. My Luke. My love. Sometimes he cries after we make love.

Sylvie, Oxford

Sylvie, hold it there. Don't go away. You need to see this . . .

Hi,
I've just broken up with my girlfriend. We've been going out since school and it was really intense, adolescent stuff. I was the first bloke who shagged her. We did all that embarrassing kids' stuff: poetry out loud, our song, sharing clothes . . . But now we're at different universities and, frankly, it's a relief to be single. I'm excited. It's a new chapter. I don't want to have to do everything with another person. She could be very judgemental. Look, I know she's going to write to you because she's left me 36 messages, some of them just sobbing. I've had 110 texts and emails and I've had to block her from my Facebook page. I tried to let her down gently. I don't want to hurt her and I'll always love what we had and I really do hope we can be mates. But it was school, we were 16, I need to move on. I don't want to cheat on her, but I don't want her to be the only girl I ever had sex with. Couples break up, isn't that part of being young? I'm not callous. But really, can't she get over it? Look, I'm hurting too.

Anonymous

OK, Anonymous. Or Luke as you're also known. Both of you, Luke and Sylvie. I've shown your letters round the office, at dinner parties, in the park and at a bus stop. Sorry, but you'd be amazed at the reaction: loads of nostalgia, sighs and smiles, a couple of retrieved memory tears, and everyone has a story. Reams and reams of reminiscences. The sympathy fell exactly, unerringly, along gender lines. Men thought Luke had a point. Women wanted to slap him and take Sylvie round a bottle of wine and a box set of *Sex and the City*. A couple of guys asked if I had a photograph of Sylvie. What surprised me was the empathy wasn't split between dumped and dumpees because a recent study (undertaken by me) shows there is a pattern to the end of affairs. People tend to be finishers or the finished. It seems we are either love's assassins or love's victims. And we repeat the same song over and over. We either get frightened and leave or we go deaf and blind and wait to be left. Sylvie, the conventional wisdom is a hug, a drink and rebound sex. Like herbal tea for herpes, it doesn't work. Nothing works. Your mother will tell you that time is a great healer. It isn't, it's just a lot of minutes sewn together. You don't ever get over your first love. You put a gag on it and lock it in the emotional attic. But it comes back every time you start a new relationship. It is the template of every affair. Every partnership is different and bespoke but, like suits, they're all made to a pattern that is cut out by the first one. And Luke, I'm afraid though your mates will be offering you man hugs and high fives, the same applies to you. This mildly self-pitying and justifying belief that you're missing out on something around the corner or in the next room, that the arse will always be keener, will follow you round like a shallow curse. The sorry truth is, we don't make the beds we have to lie in. Other people unmake them. There is no right or wrong here. If there were, love wardens would hand out tickets. The good news is, neither of you will get over this. You will go on doing it. You will try to medicate the symptoms until you lose the will and the urge. You won't be friends. You will lose touch. But you will always be first loves. And secretly and silently you will miss and yearn for each other, in small intensely painful ways, for the rest of your lives. Like when unguarded Auden whispers, "Lay your sleeping head, my love, Human on my faithless arm." Someone get a hankie for Sylvie. PS: Next month, I think we might run a compendium of the most frequently used or amusing dump-lines: "You know, it's not you it's me"; "I love you, I'm just not in love with you"; "I think we need to be apart for a bit so we can get closer"; "I obviously don't make you happy"; "I'm doing this for both of us". And this month's favourite: "I'm just a bad person". Unarguable and honest. Send in your best shots, either received or given, but nothing you've heard Billy Crystal say please.

Dear Uncle,
It's spring-ish. Please, what's the definitive rule on shorts?
                                                        Edgar, Soho

I'm so pleased you asked me, Ed. It's never after 12. Years, not o'clock. No 13-year-old or over should be seen in trousers that finish above the ankle. It doesn't matter how good your legs are, or if you're on a beach in Bermuda where they invented the things. This isn't about tan or temperature. This is about dignity. It is impossible to be taken seriously in shorts. No one has ever cared about anything said by a man in shorts. You can propose marriage naked or in handcuffs, but no one is going to agree to forsake all others for a man in shorts. You can't declare war in shorts or deliver a eulogy in shorts. Shorts are silly. Men in shorts are silly men. And silly is about the worst thing a man can be.

Dear AA,

Why do women complain so much? I mean it's so much better to be a woman than a man. They get everything paid for and they can have sex whenever they want. A woman can walk into a pub and shout "I fancy a fuck!" and there'll be a dozen blokes all over her. If I walked into a pub and shouted "I fancy a fuck!" I'd get my head kicked in.

Joe, by email

I could put you right on so many things, Joe. I could point out the comparative earning and career opportunities between men and women. I could draw your attention to the incidence of violence toward women and the rape statistics. But you wouldn't listen. And we both know you're right. I would just add, though, that the reason so few women do stand in the doorways of pubs shouting "I fancy a fuck!" is because they'd be pulling a dozen blokes like you out of their underwear. I'm pretty sure you don't have to say anything to get your head kicked in.

Dear Uncle,
Nobody understands me.

Charles, by email

What?

Mr Gill,

*Can you settle an argument? My mate says that girls don't like
to see a chap's todger through his strides. I, on the other hand,
know that a bit of a man bulge is a come-on. I mean, look at
Becks in his kecks. That's got to be a pull, ain't it? The only thing
is how do you arrange the cushions? I mean, a lazy lob down the
side of the Wranglers? Commando in the tracky bottoms? Or a
neat, assertive bulge up front in the chinos?*

Freddy, Carlisle

Ah, Freddy. Planning on staying a virgin for long, are we?
The reason you are writing this letter and your mate isn't
is because he's next door shagging your sister. Or is it your
mum again? One of the great disconnects between the male
and female of this species is in the perception of the aesthetic
appeal of man-gristle. Men think their little willies are pretty
handsome. And therefore women must, too. They believe
the thing is intrinsically beautiful. The clue that this might
not be a shared opinion is the obvious truth that no woman
in this history of sex has ever said, "Oh, my, what a heavenly scrotum." And girls rarely have tattoos of penises on
their forearms. The whole codpiece/penis sheath/dancer's
posing pouch thing is there to intimidate other men, not
attract women. The matador's bulge is for the benefit of

the bull. I have yet to meet a woman who doesn't think that on their own, without context, penises are risibly absurd, puffed up with their own pathetic self-importance. The true comedy of manhood is that your knob may well be the axle around which life revolves, but it is also ridiculously stupid.

Sir/Madam,

I think I'm a Liberal. I've always been attracted to proportional representation and closer ties to Europe, but I can't talk to anyone about it. My parents are missionary position Labour. My dad says Liberals should be shot and my mum thinks they're just Tories who don't like being spanked. I know my friends would laugh at me. And what girl's going to go out with a Liberal? So I pretend to be an anarchist. But I feel like a fraud. My heart's with a caring, devolved society and a fiscally responsible mixed economy, with checks and balances and no nuclear deterrent. What shall I do? I'm marginally desperate.

Sam, by email

Sam, there are those who think Liberalism is a mental disorder and can be cured. They might suggest you try fox hunting, running a hedge fund and listening to thrash metal. You could go into treatment, do aversion therapy by spending six weeks in Finland, but personally I don't hold with that. I think you're born Liberal and I don't see any reason why you shouldn't marry or adopt children. You don't have to tell everyone straight away, you can have proportional coming out. You might start just by trying to tell the truth and not saying what you think other people want to hear. And stop smiling in that insincere way and do something about your

67

sweaty hands. For more advice, get in touch with my helpline: *twofacedscab@torybumboy.yuk.*

Dear Uncle,

I work as a temp. Six months ago, I was sent to do reception and secretarial for an import/export company in south London. It's a bit fly by night, above an estate agent. There's just me and my boss. He's not really my type. The first week was quite normal, then I came in to find a crucifix and a lot of small bones on my desk. My boss told me to drink some tea; it tasted bitter. Then he spat on my cardie. Now I'm his sex slave. He says I'm inhabited by evil spirits. He has sex with me up to five times a day while I carry on with the work. I don't believe in this black magic mumbo jumbo but I'm powerless to resist. How can I stop this happening? I'm supposed to be going away with the kids to Lakeland next week.

June, by email

June, all advice columnists have a folder marked "Nutters, Flashers and Kardashians". Normally your letter would be a shoo-in, but there's something about it that makes me pretend it's normal. I'm fascinated by psychic, spiritual, otherworldy coercion. There's a man who writes every week to ask me if you can catch STDs from extraterrestrial rectal probes, as if the only thing that questing aliens will want to do when they finally discover sentient life in the galaxy is look up the arse of a retired diversity outreach coordinator from Kirklees. I mean, just imagine if we got to Mars and discovered warm-blooded life, what would we do? Actually, if it had more than one orifice, we'd probably shag it. (Especially if we were Russians.) You just would, wouldn't you? For the bragging rights: "You'll never guess where this has been." Sorry, this isn't helping. June, you may not believe in this "mumbo jumbo", though I should draw your attention to the dichotomy that it is pulling your knickers to one side. But your boss does. What seems to be his supernatural strength is in fact his weakness. You just have to be a better witch doctor than him. Get in early, sprinkle blood on his chair, tie a tampon to the phone, put a black cockerel in his drawer, make a votive voodoo doll out of wax, belly button fluff and bogeys (get the kids to help). Appear with a distant smile and break off conversations to swear in a baritone voice. Burn the eyes out of photographs. Write random Swedish words on the wall in soot. Pop an Alka-Seltzer in your mouth: it makes very convincing froth. And bark like a rutting fox. He will be putty in the hands of your demonic possession. I suggest you take over the business, make him your apprentice bitch. You haven't mentioned what it is you both do, but I'm assuming it involves internally stuffed drug mules from west Africa and the usual "I'll share my $50,000,000 with you please send bank details". Of course you can go on shagging the poor dupe, but over his desk rather than yours.

❖   ❖   ❖

Dear Sir,

I'm a stand-up comedian. I do observational monologues rather than tell jokes. My act takes a great deal of time to work out. The humour is often oblique, making unexpected cultural references that grow on the audience. The thing is, I suffer from hecklers. If someone shouts out from the audience, I'm thrown. And the narrative bond with them is broken. I'm not an aggressive or combative performer. I tried reasoning with them, pleading. I've even tried paying them (that got the biggest laugh of the gig). I've developed dreadful stage fright. And eczema. All I ever wanted to do was be a comedian. Please, please help me.

Paddy, London

You're shit and you know you are, you're shit and you know you are, you're shit and you know you are . . . LOL

AA,

I'm really, really excited about outdoor sex. My girlfriend says we should try everything. What do you recommend?

Tom, by email

Tom, the world's your oyster. I'm not sure how qualified I am as an erotic tour guide. I'm assuming you and your girlfriend are just setting out on life's sexual pilgrimage. All the kit is still new and shiny, a little stiff, a bit tight, and you're both dewy thighed about it all. I don't want to be a party pooper, but then poop and parties pretty much go together. Most of the things you think you want to do aren't anything like as much fun as they're cracked up to be. All the stuff they get up to in porn movies, it's like doing an assault course while desperately trying to think of Megan Fox. Most of the people who regularly have sex under the stars do it because they don't have an indoors to go to. Doggers are homeless wife swappers. Outside, you may have noticed, doesn't have a roof. It's cold, wet, hard, lumpy and dirty, none of it in a good way. There are some places that should be sued under the sex descriptions act. Attempting coitus in a jacuzzi is the most overrated and unpleasant experience in all of civilisation. Sex on a beach is cold, clammy and uncomfortable; you really don't want sand up

72

there. Sex in the sea is impossible unless you're the passive partner of a dolphin. I do, though, recommend sex in a tent: half inside, half outside. Or a balmy veranda in Provence. The floor of a box in the Royal Albert Hall during Elgar's Cello Concerto worked very well for me once. Sex is about physics and engineering. It's simple. Bridge and tunnel. Love is different. You can have the best sex of your life anywhere if it's with the right person at the right moment. Wherever you do it, all sex is inside.

Dear AA,

I'm in love with a fantastic girl and we're thinking of taking it to the next level: moving in together with the option of marriage, kids, the whole nine in-laws. The trouble is, she believes in fairies. I'm embarrassed just writing it. Suzie's perfectly rational in every other way. She trained as a lawyer, she works for a charity, has a nice, agnostic family, isn't superstitious, just adamantly believes in fairies. They're fucking everywhere. Hiding the car keys, bringing luck, looking after special places. It makes me so mad. I get unpleasant, make jokes in public, and tease her. I know it's unkind, but fuck it, she believes in fucking fairies. How can I convince her the goblins have eaten them all? My future depends on it.

Rob, by email

Indeed, Rob, it probably does. At the moment your future looks decidedly pixie-lated. Let's step back. You believe in football, don't you? Ah, you riposte, but football is real; everyone else can see it too. True. But is your belief rational? Is crying over the achievements or failures of men you don't know normal? Is the votive belief in signed T-shirts and hallowed turf sensible? Is hating other people because they love 11 different footballers? Is putting off sex to listen to Alan Hansen the behaviour of a rational human being?

74

You see, Rob, it's not what you believe. It can be transubstantiation, Genesis, the divine right of kings, the free market, Bolton Wanderers, or fairies. What matters is how you believe it. Does it make you a better, more empathetic, kinder, more charitable human being? Or does it make you worse? Now I gather that the girlfriend is charming, clever, decent, imaginative and long-suffering. Because it's not fairies you don't believe in, it's Suzie. If you love someone, you do it because of what they are, not despite it. She loves you with the football. That almost certainly makes you a less attractive man. And as we speak, the little people are probably whispering in her ear that you are a judgemental, earthbound, self-reverential, unimaginative, selfish twat. And the stork's never coming anywhere near you.

Dearest Uncle D,
I couldn't ever love a Tory.

Jocasta, Gloucestershire

Quite right. You don't want to go breeding with Tories. No one loves a Conservative, particularly other Conservatives. To be a Tory is the antonym of lovable. They're there to make the world safe and comfortable and solvent, so that other people who aren't Tories can have sex in a land fit for Lefties. That's the terrible dichotomy of Conservatism. If you want lovable, go and grab a Green Party member. They all fucking ooze lovability 24/7.

Sir,
My girlfriend says size doesn't matter. Is she right?

Peter, by email

She's right. She's right for you, wee man. She's a thoughtful liar. Put it this way: in which other area or aspect of your life does size not matter? Is a double the same as a single? Is a three-room flat the same price as a one-room flat? Is horsepower all in Clarkson's imagination? Would you not give a fig if your holiday were 10 instead of 14 days? Or your girlfriend 14 instead of eight stone? Exactly. So do you really think the only thing in the world where size doesn't matter is your peepee?

Dear Uncle,

I've just discovered my fiancé is shagging a girl I've asked to be a bridesmaid. We're supposed to be getting married next month. What surprised me wasn't that he'd hump the sad, stupid, diseased little tart, but that I don't feel heartbroken. I'm not in bits, I'm not devastated, there is no sobbing. I am not writing this from a humiliated pool of desolate rejection. I am cool and focused. I am steely and smiley. But mostly, I am furious. Incandescently, levitatingly, titanically, stratospherically, scorched-earth angry. I am so angry I could sack a city. I am angry enough to become a child's dentist. I could stamp on kittens in stilettos (me, not the kittens). I am so angry I could tweet. But I am also contained. He doesn't know I know. Like a thermos, I am cold on the outside; inside I'm a meltdown of boiling broccoli and stilton. I don't want your pity, or caring strategies for coping. I don't need homilies on forgiveness. I want vengeance. And you are obviously a fickle and twisted man. I'd bet you've taken a loved-one's trust and cynically used it to seduce another. You've looked into a partner's eyes and lied into her teeth. So I need you to tell me what will really hurt. What will inflict the most agonising and lasting damage. I want his entire existence to be bitter gall and wormwood. I need him humiliated and ridiculed. The rest of his life must be a long and bleak plodding repetition of remorse, punctuated with bouts of

78

incapacitating self-pity. For him, happiness must be a stone in the shoe that momentarily takes his mind from what a fucking monumental cunt-struck irredeemable tragedy he's made of his sorry existence.

Fiona, by email

Marry him.

Dear AA,
I'm bored.

Matthew, by email

Ah, the authentic siren call of civilisation's descent into
decadence. Of course you're bored. Everyone you know is
bored. You've been bored since you could fling Lego.
Boredom is the waste product of choice. The more there is
on offer, the more you don't want. Fifty options of cereal
does not hone an epicurean expertise in the finer points of
puffed rice, it murders appetite. Boredom is not a thing. It's
not a feeling or a condition. Boredom is the echo in an
empty box, a single glove, the sound of an abandoned piano.
It can also be a calling, a hobby. People collect boredom,
they hoard it, they wallow in it, hoping that one day it'll be
of interest and become an effete ennui. Let me tell you, it
doesn't. Boredom is an addiction without a high, a disease
without a symptom. I once had it. I would say I suffered
from it, but you don't suffer boredom. That would be interesting, or at least engaging. And then something interesting
happened, or at least the promise of something interesting.
I was at a party I didn't want to be at, as usual standing in
a corner with a look of ineffable disinterest, and as usual I
was being droned at by a man who was either writing a

thesis on Colette or about to go potholing in Cheshire. When, blessedly, his bladder finally called him away, an old girlfriend who I'd become tired of sauntered over and asked how I was. I said I was being bored, without the option of death, by the Pope of Bores. "Yes," she said, "I was watching. Only one of you was bored. He was having a wonderful time. Animated, expansive, discursive, verbose. He was entertaining himself royally. In fact, he was having so much fun I see he's on his way back." And in that moment I had an epiphany. Perhaps epiphany is a little too interesting. It was a spark of understanding. Just as the great panjandrum of boring got back into the saddle to once more scale the foothills of French literature, or bird table etiquette, I held up a limp hand and whispered, "Before we once again embark on this treadmill of loquacity, perhaps you could spare me a couple of minutes to explain how it was you became such an accomplished and polished bore. Please, don't spare me a single detail." The chap looked first startled, and then his eyes narrowed and one eyebrow arched knowingly. A smile flickered over his wet lips and he turned and walked away without uttering a word. And for the first time in, ooh, a great many grey years, I felt elated. I buttonholed the old girlfriend and said, "Let's get out of here. I have something very exciting to tell you." "Oh, couldn't we just have sex instead?" she replied. And from that day on, I have devoted myself to being a bore. Not just any old bore. Not just a common or garden, end-of-the-bar bore. But the greatest bore that ever lived. I wake each morning quivering and alive with the joy of the hunt to find new things to bore on about. Sometimes I forget to eat I'm so entranced with boredom. There are so few subjects I can't bore on about at length, with footnotes. And I am asked to bore professionally. My boringness is a regular fixture at the literary festival at Hay. Just last week, I was boring schoolteachers at Wellington College's Education Weekend: a tricky professional audience, but I think I ground them down. Oh! And what's this? Look here, I've been boring on about boredom for over 800 words and you're thinking, is there no end to this answer? But you see, I get paid by the word, so whilst you've been sitting there thinking, "Oh, get on with it!" I've made [editor-redacted sum] and enjoyed myself enormously. So let this be a lesson to you. If you're bored, it's because someone else is fulfilling his dream. Become a bore. It's the most interesting thing you'll ever do.

Sir,

I'm getting a little portly. But I fancy I still cut something of an elegant dash. Can I sport a cummerbund?

Lionel, Hampshire

Of course you can. You could also sport tasselled nipple clamps, a barbed-wire cock ring and a peacock feather butt plug. What you're asking is: will people think me a fine and well-dressed fellow in a cummerbund? And the answer is, probably not. In fact, the only people who will ever appreciate you in a cummerbund are other men in cummerbunds. The sight of a similarly accoutred fat bloke will give them a sense of relief that they have turned up dressed correctly. Cummerbunds are the dinner dance equivalent of tasselled nipple clamps in a convent. Cummerbunds were first adopted by Indian Army officers stationed on the North-West Frontier, where they would wrap the turbans of their troopers round their waists. The military fashion spread round the world. The French Foreign Legion still wear cummerbunds as part of their dress uniform. The word cummerbund comes from Hindi. Or, more probably, Hindustani, the military pidgin language used in India. It means loincloth. Before that it possibly originated in Persian . . . Sorry I think this is supposed to be part of the answer to the previous question.

Dear Sir,

Last month, I read an article in Esquire *about the woman's view of a well-dressed man and I haven't been able to leave the house since. It was rough. I'm standing naked on a pile of my so-called clothes. I don't even know what pants to put on any more.*

Colin, by email

We are now all imagining you nakedly waiting for this month's *Esquire* to land on your mat so you can shiveringly flick through the pages to see if there's an answer and you can get dressed. Well, there is. But not so fast, shrivel dick. Before we get to what looks good on you, let's spend a moment on what looks good about you. Most men spend far longer looking at their clothes than they do at themselves. Go and stand in front of the mirror and have a forensic gander. Now breathe out and do it again. No man has ever seen himself breathing out. Now pretend you're a potentially hot date. What is it about you that's make or break? Ignore the things you can't change. You can't be taller, and you can't change the colour of your eyes. What are you going to do about the other stuff? For instance, do you have any idea how hairy your arse really is? Before you worry about trouser length and colour blocking, have a look at your toenails. If there is only one piece of advice I'd give to you it's have a pedicure. Really. Nice feet go a long way. (And if you're a chiropodist, I'll give you that as your slogan.) As for the rest of the schumtter, men's clothes have nothing to do with fashion or style or even tradition. All the blokes in the article you mention were good-looking to begin with. Jean-Paul Belmondo, Marlon Brando, Ryan Gosling, Jon Hamm: they're dudes who make clothes look good, not who are made to look good by their clothes. Cary Grant looks wonderful in his Anderson & Sheppard suits. You could put Rab C Nesbitt in one and he'd still be Rab C Nesbitt only in a really good suit. I'm going to make this simple, because I realise you're cold. There are only two words you need to remember. You could have them tattooed on your knuckles, but only if you had 11 fingers on one hand and four on the other. They are "nonchalance" and "elan". The problem is they are usually mutually exclusive, but you need to dress with elan and wear your clothes with nonchalance. How you wear is more important than what you wear. The worst dressed man in any room is the one who won't order spaghetti because he's got an Hermès tie on.

To Uncle Dysfunctional,

My best mate is going to ask his girlfriend to marry him. I think it's a mistake. She's a fit bird, but she's a flirt. I know she'll cheat on him – she's always giving me the eye. He says I'm being overprotective. We've been best mates since infant school. He'd trust her with his life. So I said, I'll prove it. And to make it more interesting, let's put a grand on it. Anyway, I've got to go into hospital for a routine hernia, but I've told her it's cancer of the bollocks. And I've only got a couple of months. And that I'll never have sex again. And I begged her to come down to the hospital to help me out with one last how's-your-father just as me best mate's mate. And then I'll arrange for my mate to find her there, prove the point. Knacker the nuptials, collect a grand. Job's a good'un.

Dwayne, East London

Dear Adrian,

This may seem like an odd question. I'm engaged to a really great guy. We're getting married in the autumn. The only problem is his best man. They've been friends since the sandpit. The thing is, my man has outgrown him. The guy's a real loser. He's also a creepy letch who's always trying to touch me up. But my fiancé's too nice to move on. Anyway, the "best friend" has to go into hospital for something embarrassing. And all larky,

86

he's asked me to go and give him a handjob for £500. He's such a sordid creep. But I'm planning on going ahead, getting the money up front and then having my boyfriend come in and catch him.

Holly, Shoreditch

Mate:
I'm getting married to this great girl. There's only one problem. My best man and her don't get on. It really upsets me that the two people I love most in the world can't see how brilliant each other is. I've arranged for them to be in hospital at the same time so they can spend some time together and see what really matters. They both think I'll be there but I won't. I know this sounds desperate but it's really important to me as time is short. My mate thinks he's got a hernia. But really it's a terminal tumour. I really want him to be happy and find peace before he dies.

Graham, London

Nothing I can say will improve the perfect circular tragedy that you've all cleverly made out of your lives. Let me guess: you all studied Jacobean drama at university.

Dearest Adrian,
Why can't everyone just be happy?

Rufus, by email

The world is divided between those who read your question and said, "What a good question! We could all be happy if we were all really nice. And if we were happy we wouldn't be so ambitious. We'd just be satisfied with what we had and we'd share with others and make them happy, too. And their happiness would make us more happy. And we could all get happier and happier until we were in a mutually happy inflation of smiles. That would carry on to escalating bliss because everyone knows that happiness is catching; happy begats happy." But on the other hand, there are those who read your question and thought, "You dope-addled, hippy dipshit. Of course everyone can't be happy because if they were, happiness would be meaningless. We'd be happy when our kittens died. Our friends would be happy at our cancer of the bollocks. Mums and dads would be happy when the kids fell into the canal, strapped into their pushchairs with a smiley nanny who can't swim or shout 'Help!' in English. We'd be happy at earthquakes and Ebola and Vin Diesel box sets. We would live in a syrup of happiness." Everything that is worth having or doing is made or inspired by unhappiness, ranging from unease to abject misery. And the least you need to run a civilisation is a sense that things could be better. But the real reason we can't all be happy is because the second lot of people are going to make the first lot of people really miserable. There is nothing as attractive as a happy person and nothing more infuriating than their happiness. The most unedifying and secret guilty pleasure of a dystopian life is taking away the happiness of someone else. Happy people, of course, are blind to anything but kittens and moonbeams. They never see the miserable thief in the night. Now you can tell from this answer I'm not one of life's Pollyannas. But, then again, neither do I believe we are designed to be disappointed and depressed. Protestantism came up with the idea of original sin. If you take it out of the Garden of Eden, you can see it as being a human default setting of self-interest, which is constantly uncomfortable and which in turn sets us to strive for happiness. It's like fishing. You bait your hook with good intentions and hope, and you sit around moaning and bitching and every so often you get a tug at the end of the line and it's happy. And you hold it for a bit and have your picture taken and then you put it back and go on complaining and getting wet. And after a bit, when you've caught happy a few times, you realise that what you're really after, what actually sustains you, is the anticipation. The happy in happiness is the expectation of happiness. Of course, if you kill the fish and eat it, it's just fish and you'll probably get a bone in your throat.

89

Sir,

Isn't it true that human females are the only animals that have orgasms? And seeing as nature made sex so colossally brilliant – seeing as even after a gazillion years of civilisation and all the technology and ingenuity of millions and millions of people, we've yet to come up with anything that's remotely as good or that we'd rather do – how come we don't do it all the time, with everyone? I read that most women say they've slept with, like, four or five people in their lives. Why not thousands? Why don't people give each other sex for fun? Why aren't we doing it in queues, on the bus, in Starbucks? Why did we take the best thing we've ever been given, the thing that costs nothing, that is the most mood-enhancing feeling in the history of the universe and cover it in guilt and embarrassment and all sorts of weird religious rules and conventions and superstitions? Why don't we all just get together and rethink the whole thing? And just go, "Fuck it, let's get laid"?

Gus, by email

Hi, Gus. I'm guessing you're not getting any. You've got no fingerprints on your right hand and the little peepee's got a pistol grip. I'm sorry to have to tell you this: it is only you. Everyone else is having sex all the time with everyone else except you. We weren't going to say, but now you've asked. You see, if we did take you up on your idea – which frankly, on the face of it, in a men's magazine, has its attractions – you still wouldn't be getting laid. Because sex isn't like PE. Everyone doesn't have to do it twice a week with a double period on Fridays. If we did decide to start humping like chimps, it would still be the alpha males and the prettiest females who got rogered rotten while the best you and your friend Derek could hope for would be a ritual buggering from a big bully as some submissive humiliation thing. Lady chimps would also say they've only had sex with four or five people. It's just the same four or five people for all of them. Sex is never going to be fair and even all the stuff you complain about – the secrecy, the religious morality, the jealousy, the guilt, the yearning, well, actually, that's what makes sex sexy. Without all that it's just hands-free wanking – which may sound good to you at the moment but is not the real deal. Sex is about the expectation, the look, the whisper, the hint, the sniff, the promise. That's what makes it the best thing ever invented. And let me tell you something about chimpworld, jungle erotics. Chimpanzees have smaller penises than humans, relative to their size. But they have huge balls. Really impressive, bow-legged orbs of generation. The reason is that their sex is perfunctory, rudimentary and fretful. You never know who's coming up behind you. What Cheetah needs is not technique but spunk. Chimpanzees produce copious amounts of shoot-juice. They need it to wash out all the previously deposited effluvia from the other guys in the band. Chimps don't go in for a lot of oral sex and that's something to be borne in mind before we engage in your whoopee free-for-all global gangbang. The prime directive still remains. Sex is driven by genes. The pleasure is the packaging. They don't really care if you like it or not. They just need to know they're not sharing a womb. And here, incidentally, is your bonus fun fact: the ridge at the bottom of your bell end (or in your case the ridge that used to be at the bottom of your bell end), may have been designed as an airtight plunger to extract competing sperm from your partner's vagina. Like a bicycle pump. Try slipping that into your precoital pillow talk, if you ever get that far.

Dear Uncle,

I really love sex. Really, really love it. I can't get enough of it. I love the anticipation, the flirting, the seduction, the first touch of hands, the moment when a kiss turns from a peck into a snog, and a hand sliding down a back and a shrug of a jacket and the clasp of a bra and the warm hard nipples pressed against my chest, the ... oh shit, oh shit, sorry, fuck, sorry, that's never happened before... Oh, except of course it has, it happens every time. I have a real problem with premature ejaculation. I hate this useless hysterical knob, it's like having Alan Sugar in your pants, always exploding too soon and inappropriately – and they look rather similar. To make matters worse there is so much of it, and it seems to be fired from some medieval siege engine. There's jiz everywhere and ...

Jason, by email

OK, Jason, we're going to have to cut it there. Too much warm, sticky information all over the breakfast table, thank you. This month's column is going to be devoted to positive thinking, turning the "oh nos" into "oh yeses", seeing that half-empty glass as half-full, or in your case, half-spilt. Let's look at premature ejaculation. A sideways look, obviously. Take these two words: only one of them is a problem – premature. It's the premature bit we want to cure. The ejaculating seems to be working fine, like the end of a Grand Prix. Premature just means "too soon". So it all depends on when you begin. Don't get the big guns out at the first squeal. Give your partner a head start – and that is a double entendre. Give her a hand: she's a girl, so she can go round a couple of laps and you'll catch her up later, bringing up the rear. Produce the Sugar man for the grand finale; she'll be impressed by the pyrotechnics if not the technique. And you did say that anticipation is everything. In the end – and that's another innuendo – sex is selfish, and just as you are only worried about your outcome, so is she. The thing you both care about is that you come second. And remember: if women could have premature ejaculation, they'd all want one, and there'd be sister workshops on how to get there faster.

Dear AA,

I just got a new girlfriend and she's great. We get on well, have a laugh, we like the same music, films, books and stuff. The thing is she's got politics, loads and loads of them. I had no idea someone could get angry about that much. She's got opinions where I don't have thoughts. She's sort of lefty, I think. I'm not really interested. My family always voted Conservative, so we're not really into politics and stuff. I always thought it was like taking an interest in street sweeping or railway timetables, but her lot are really into it. They argue about it and if I try and lighten it up, tell a joke and say "who gives a shit, let's have a drink", they all glare at me. And now she's saying she doesn't know if she can commit to someone who doesn't care about the world, and the plight of the workers and badgers and immigrants and kids and roads and the environment and the Middle East and pensions and the disestablished Church, and what should I do? Should I just fake it and pretend to worry about Colombian peasants every time I pop into Costa?

George, Bolton

The short answer is yes, but you need to convert swiftly. You'll need to do a bit of research, a bit of reading, but you can just get most of your convictions off Wikipedia. You'll notice that politics is not really about being for things, because

95

everybody wants the same things; it's about being against stuff, so you need to learn to recognise the things you're against: public schools, men in ties, semi-detached houses with double-drives, banks, plastic surgery, boxing, Elgar, flags but not banners, champagne, the missionary position and Switzerland. It's not difficult. And then you have to be really, really strident about it – go on and on and on. And to begin with she'll be thrilled, then after about a week of you banging on about the plight of Kashmir and the shameful lack of micro-loans for Malawian women's collectives, she'll show signs of getting fed up. No one likes to be out-leftied, and after a couple of weeks she'll start suggesting you give the politics a rest and get drunk and have sloppy sex instead. You'll think that's it, that you've won and that you can go back to being a normal, ignorant cynical slob. Well you can't. She's just getting ready to slam you with the next thing, which is likely to be vegetarianism or 19th-century literature. Be prepared for "I could never sleep with anyone who hasn't read *Madame Bovary*."

Dear Uncle Dysfunctional,

My fiancée – my ex-fiancée – got hold of my phone and went through all my texts and emails. She discovered what she calls "inappropriate messages and behaviour": a bit of harmless flirting and some bloke has resent me a pic of his mate's mate's girlfriend wearing a Queen mask with her tits out. You couldn't even rattle one off the wrist over Her Maj, no matter how perky her top bollocks were. A bit of banter with mates about rows we'd had and a great weekend getting drunk with bum sex. You know, all the stuff blokes talk about. Well, she hit the Artex, accused me of not being straight and open and, of course, out of a clear blue Sunday, apropos of nada, taken off guard, I went on the offensive. I pointed out how bloody dare she go through my personal stuff and she'd crossed a line and it was deceitful and underhand, and by this time we were both yelling and simultaneously shouted, "If there's no trust in this relationship we'd better call it a fucking day!" Then there was a stunned silence and we haven't spoken for a week. I've let it be known that if she says sorry I'll forgive and forget: clean sheet. She sent a message that if I apologise on my knees in tears in front of all her mates she'll think about having me back. I'm right though, aren't I?

Tony, London

Well, Tony, up to a point. That is, actually, in practical terms, no you're not. Let's look at where you stand. At this precise moment you're engaged to your right hand and a mobile phone. How right does that feel to you? What we have here is a very fine example of double standards. Double like apartheid; that is, parallel and different. Men and women understand different things about personal boundaries. What men call privacy, women know as secrecy. So while you think of your phone as being the modern equivalent of a gent's study or shed – a sacrosanct place where you can mooch about with one hand down your trackies collecting things in old tobacco tins and writing dribbly memoirs – you imagine that it's a space that is yours alone. What you look at or giggle over is fine as long as it stays in the shed. Women, on the other hand, will think that that's self-serving bollocks. They're right. That doesn't make it wrong, it just makes it self-serving bollocks. It's a thought crime, you see. Men think the action is what's wrong. Women think it's the intent. If you want to get legal about it, they're both crimes. You imagine privacy is a vital part of a relationship. What happens in the bathroom and on the internet stays in the bathroom and on the internet. She thinks its duplicitous, secretive and humiliating. But here's the thing: if you said, "I'm just going upstairs to describe the sex we had last night to my mate Ron, and then Skype my ex in the bath," she'd say, "Don't forget to mention that I came three times and tell me if Shirley still has one tit lower than the other." But if in return she said, "I'm going out to have a drink with the girls and will be mentioning your cutie ickle-wickle cock, then I'm gonna have dinner with a bloke who once asked me out before I met you but I wasn't interested," you'd sulk for a week.

For men, privacy means not being told stuff that would hurt. For women, secrecy is having stuff go on behind your back. So call all her mates, make a date, get down on your knees and snivel. Because whilst you're both right, she's righter than you. And always will be.

Dear Unc,

I'm a photographer. I specialise in portraits and glamour work. Nothing seedy, it's all tasteful and sophisticated rather than raunchy. I was taking a series of snaps of girls in classic Sapphic poses and, as I was checking them on the computer, my lady-friend had a gander and exclaimed, "Christ! She's got a weird vadge." "Who?" I said. "What do you mean, 'Who?' The one with the deformed trumpet." "Deformed?" I said. "I can't tell the difference." Well, that tore it. "You can't tell the difference between a perfectly normal growler and Quasimingo?" Then she got her book group involved. And they all agreed that one of the girls had a kebab that belonged in a medical museum. But bugger me if I could see why. They kept explaining but it was like listening to people shout the instructions for folding ornamental napkins.

Leon, by email

Before I give an answer, I'm going to run the next letter, which is related . . .

Uncle D,

How do you address a new snatch? What do you call it? I pulled this bird the other night and we were getting down to the main course and I said, by way of encouragement, "Oi! Let the dog see the rabbit!" Next thing I'm standing on the wrong side of the front door wearing my trousers as a snood. What was I supposed to say? And don't write "vagina". I can barely type "vagina".

Jack, Manchester

Funnily, neither can my iPad. It's just tried to spell-check it as "Virginia", "Virgoan", "virgin" or "Virginian". You could always try Virginia. In answer to both of you, the mons veneris, pudenda, labia both minor and major, perineum and clitoris will always be names on a map of a place we visit but are strangers to, a destination of which we know little though we have often gone down for the weekend. It is another country, and we don't speak Cuntish. Jack, I sympathise. They're pretty much all much of a muchness. They look the same, the way pastrami sandwiches all look the same. The ladygarden isn't a delicate yielding place of fey petals in subtly dusty hues scented with musk and oud. It's a mess. A lovely mess, a boy's own mess, but it's an edible laundry basket that was made in the dark by a gay God. And as for what you call it, best to wait to be introduced. You could try the creepily paternalistic opening, "Oh, and who do we have here?" If you think that'll set the wrong tone, just leap in with, "Wow! You have one round the front as well!" Or you might like to introduce yours first. "Say hello to Mr Ruff Puff." Or, "Meet Throb the Babymaker". In the hope that she'll say, "Pleased to meet you, I'm sure. This is secret Num-num Hideyhole." Or, "The Toothless Cock Muncher". But be warned. There are plenty of girls for whom a baptised penis is a deal breaker. Groaning, "Hey, bitch, beg Mr Muscle for more!" is a rare turn-on that won't work for everyone. The naming of parts is one of the lacunae of language. Mind you, lacunae isn't a bad name for it. It's not that we lack colloquial terms for the organs of reproduction, it's just that there are precious few that sound affectionate. So we're going to start a competition for the best his and her names for the moist bits. The prize will be something suitably euphemistic donated by a major *Esquire* advertiser. We might also have a runner-up prize for the worst names, the ones that are least likely to get you a cooked breakfast. Like, Wizard's Sleeve, Pottyhole, Splosh or – my most-least favourite – Slimepocket.

Dear Nuncy Dysfuncy,
I really, really fancy my fiancé's father. The thing is he's also my
best friend's dad. And my mother's boss. And his wife's dying of
cancer. And he's my family doctor. Do you think it's worth having
a quick no-strings how's-your-father?

Sheila, Newcastle

Yeah, go on.

Dear Uncle Dysfunctional,

I lie. Actually to be honest I don't lie. Never told a fib. On the kiddies' heads and the grave of my saint of a mother. Actually, I haven't got any kids and my mum's a slag. She's not really a slag, I don't know why I said that. See? That's what I mean. Or don't mean. I don't know why I tell lies all the time. Not all the time, obviously. At the moment, I'm flying in my Learjet to the Caribbean dictating this letter to Erica, the naked stewardess. I insist all my staff are naked above 10,000ft. You see, that's not exactly the truth. We're going to the south of France, not the Caribbean. The thing is, my girlfriend, who I love with all my heart, honest to God, cross my heart and hope to die, says she doesn't believe me and I'm planning on asking her to marry me and I know she'll just laugh and say pull the other one Penisocchio. That's what she calls me, because she says I tell lies to get laid. Which is obviously a lie. Or not.

Jake, Newcastle

Hi Jake, nice to hear from you. See what I just did there? I told a lie. On a sliding scale of things that are nice, hearing from you doesn't even register. Only we don't call that lying. We lie about it and call it manners. Politeness is the polite word for porkies. Lies are the grease that allows culture's wheels to spin without too much friction. So you say that she looks lovely in the frock when in fact she looks like something from Wayne Rooney's wank bank, because you need to get out of the house. You say the soup is delicious because you don't want to hurt your mum's feelings. You swear the dog ate your homework, you've got a dentist appointment and that you don't mind taking out the rubbish, because that's how we make life bearable. As a species, we lied before we could speak. Fibs are one of the types of communication we share with the birds and the bees. In the Kalahari, there's a juvenile lizard that imitates the look and swagger of a bombardier beetle because nobody fucks with a bombardier beetle, but everybody fucks with a kid lizard. Flowers pretend to be insects and insects flowers. Everything lies. The moon doesn't shine, it just nicks the sun's light. Without lies it would all come to a grinding, tearful, furious, depressed, murderous halt. All of it: nature, evolution, the nation state, Netflix, everything is balanced on a judicious foundation of self-serving edited truths and wishful thinking. In other words – lies. But that's not what you're really talking about. What you're worried about is trust. You lie so badly, so childishly, so amateurishly that you've spent all the capital in the trust bank. Even infant lizards lie better than you. The girlfriend doesn't trust what you say. You see, grown ups lie to promote trust. She doesn't expect that you'll be on her side and support her all the time. It's not the lies she minds, it's that you're such a bad liar. She can't trust you to lie for the common good. The one thing all compulsively bad liars have in common is that they're certain they are the only people in the room telling fibs. You think you have a monopoly on lies. Well, wake up and smell the mendacity. Of course, she knows you're a vain fantasist. And she's still around. She'll make a joke of the proposal because she doesn't want to marry you. She gets something transient out of this relationship. Dinner, holidays, access to people more interesting and sophisticated than you. But she's not serious about it. She doesn't love you. And that's the truth. But on the plus side, Penisocchio is a brilliant todger moniker. We'll keep that one, thank you very much. (I don't really mean very much, or indeed thank you.)

Mr Gill,

A parent from the school my 10-year-old son goes to rang up to say that he'd been flashing at the girls. It's not a one-off thing, he does it quite a lot. I was really shocked, there's nothing like that at home. So I made some discreet enquiries and it appears – well, it appears quite often – he can't keep his pants on. He puts on little shows of penis puppetry in the changing room, and I'm told the other kids call him Harry Hill. He's circumcised, but he's quite popular. As yet no one's made an official complaint, as he's only a child. But in a year or two he's going to be going through puberty and I really don't want him exposing himself with hair on. I'm worried sick. Is he going to grow up to be Jimmy Savile, or worse? I haven't spoken to him yet. I don't know how to tackle it. I've tried talking to his father. He just said, "It's only a little thing." And laughed.

Julie, by email

Julie, I understand this is worrying. There are two things here. First, the need for children to gain attention. It's a dog-kick-the-shit-out-of-dog world in junior school. Peer appreciation is paramount. Some play football, some tell jokes, some get their willies out. You've got to ask yourself: would you rather he was an exhibitionist or a bully, getting kudos by shoplifting and doing donuts in stolen minicabs?

107

It seems he's found a clever way to grab attention and it'll all be quite different naturally when puberty hits not just him, but the girls, too. He really won't get the same reaction of amused curiosity, and I've yet to meet a 13-year-old boy who wasn't as modest as a medieval Irish nun. The second thing is the wee knobby itself. I suggest you give the boy a mobile phone and introduce him to sexting. Possibly get his dad or a cousin to do this. This is a universally accepted form of cuneiform for kids, what they call in universities a communication tool. He already has a head start, if not a hat. He can cut some shapes with his todger and strut some genital origami. You worry about him being a pervert? If you found him taking your Wellington boots on a date, that would be a perversion. Simply getting the chubby out – well, the offence is all in the eye of the beholder. Surprising old ladies in the baking aisle of Aldi with his meat and two veg will get him arrested. Running naked across Twickenham in front of 20,000 people will get him a guest appearance on *8 Out of 10 Cats*. There is a difference between flashing and flaunting. It is a lesson worth learning early. In life, always flaunt, never flash.

Sir,

I'm in love with a girl in my class. Both our parents are very old-fashioned and are keen that we get good exam results, so we can become a doctor (her) and a lawyer (me). We're not allowed to have anything to do with the opposite sex, but all we want is to have sex. We can't think about anything else. We can't keep our hands off each other, or concentrate. I'm afraid if I don't have colossal amounts of shagging I'll fail my exams. Where can we go that doesn't cost money to fuck? Toilets are so lavatorial.

Isador, Windsor

Isador, I feel for you. I'm assuming there are no large parks near you and the library is now an interactive computer citizenship inclusion drop-in centre, so I suggest you both volunteer to visit old people. There are hundreds of them, and they'd appreciate a chat and a cup of tea and are unlikely to mind if you take 20 minutes in the spare room. If you get a really demented one, they won't notice at all. And I had a friend who had a Punch and Judy show. You know, a little tent the size of a telephone box. He was always doing au pairs inside whilst waggling his hands above his head to entertain the kiddies, and shouting with a sort of strangulated gasp, "That's the way to do it!"

Dear Sir,
I think my cock tastes funny.

Rufus, Farnborough

What, did the dog pull a face?

Dear Uncle D,
Men in scarves. What's all that about?

Ali, by email

Where have you been? It's all about the scarf, man. That wrap of ridiculous ergonomically pointless cloth that looks like an ogre's foreskin through which peeps a sulky bell-end is the defining male style statement of our times. As the cloth cap of the Thirties and the ripped jeans of the Seventies were tokens of their eras, so the man scarf is the leitmotif of the second decade of the 21st century. While the cloth cap stood for worker solidarity and heads-down industrial muscle, and ripped jeans implied a tear-it-up anarchy and street style, what does the man scarf say about your generation? Really, honestly, you all look like a class of mummy's boys. "Put your scarf on if you're going out. You don't want to catch a sore throat." You look weedy, needy, neurotic, fearful and vain. That's quite a lot of a look to get out of a strip of tablecloth. Looking back through cloudy eyes from the leather armchair by the window, it seems strange that your generation has striven through so little, having been given so much, to achieve a look quite so incapable and lost, so quiveringly tearful. You are a troupe of self-made eunuchs with your naked ankles, tortured facial hair, skimpy jackets,

111

crotch tourniquet nappy trousers. You have managed to extract the male from masculine but have failed to replace it with anything sophisticated, amused or intellectual, just a vision of nerdy, pale victimhood. The man scarf is your banner, your flag of sexual surrender. Appropriately and predictably, there are internet sites devoted to showing you how to wear your scarf, because really it's that complicated. In all the whirl of bedroom mirror variations, none of them suggests a noose at one end and tying the other to the bannister. Look, I don't care one way or the other, I've got my cravat to live up to.

Unc Dysfunc,
Why is it that when people say, "I don't want to sound bigoted",
they always do?

Carsten, Denmark

I don't know if English is the only language where some expressions only and solely mean the opposite of what they say but we do have an awful lot of them. It is something to do with our natural desire to be stridently rude while at the same time remaining smilingly polite. My favourites are: "This isn't a criticism." Oh, yes, it is. "I don't mean to be awkward . . ." You were just born that way. "It's not you, it's me." It's definitely you. "Sorry." The only thing I'm sorry about is I didn't do it harder. "Call me old-fashioned." I'm calling you an immoral slut. "Would anyone mind if . . ." If any of you mind, keep it to yourselves. "It's only a game." This is war. "Let's do lunch." I'd rather share a lolly in a sauna with Stuart Hall. "We were spellbound." Only a witch's curse kept us in our seats. "I've never done this before." I taught all your mates and your dad how to do this.

❖ ❖ ❖

113

Instead of answering yet another letter, for a change, I've decided to answer some non-specific though pressing questions of the type you commonly hear in pubs and nightclubs, hospital queues and works canteens. Do works canteens still exist? Those places with bottles of brown sauce and vinegar on Formica tables, where lathe operators and their apprentices come to eat pasties? Do lathe operators still exist? Are there still apprentices for tea, tea that is drunk strong enough to melt t'spoon, while thumbing softly greasy copies of *Tit Bits* and making ribald, explicit comments about the conical bras on the secretaries and wages clerks who are painting their nails while discussing layaway frocks and Saturday night cock? Are there still places like that, Norman? Are there? Where young Brylcreemed men with an itch for a chair in the room at the top, for cash and class, peruse *Esquire* for a glimpse of the elan that's available in pastel shades down South? Don't answer, Norman. It is a rhetorical question. We have rhetorical questions in the South.

The truth is, I'm bored. Bored, bored, bored. I want a break from your depressingly repetitive, whining, self-righteous letters. Oh, God, when you're not looking for excuses and justifications for pathetically unkind and self-serving behaviour, you're begging for better and smoother lies to attain unjustified advantages. Each new delivery is a depressing

114

litany of fearful, blinkered, furniture-humping, fickle, low expectations. No, Norman, I can't recommend a transgender nationality that has better-tasting genitals than the Brazilian ladyboys you've experienced. And not again, not for the third time, Norman, no, I don't think it's unreasonable of your wife to go off on some nancy Open University course just when you and your mates had planned your annual conga eel fishing trip, so there'll be no one there to look after your son (her stepson). And again, Norman, least said soonest mended is probably not the best option all round when you've managed to infect eight members of the same family with genital warts, including one in a coma, and added the slider of crabs. And no, Norman, it's not reasonable to ask for your money back when you discover that the telephone sex line you've been regularly patronising was in fact your wife on the extension upstairs, and that she has every right to be pissed off because you said the telephone sex with her disguised voice was better than the actual sex with her flesh.

And then to Sarah, Rachel and Camilla and the dozens of other irrepressibly half-full optimistic women who continue to write in mascara-stained tears to ask if I can suggest a sexual position or a drug that would make cohabiting bearable: no there isn't, and no I can't. Divorce the cretins, for God's sake! Walk away. Why do you all put up with expectations of men that are lower than the ones you have of Netflix? So, for this month only, Norman, I'm answering the big questions that make you look to the heavens rather than examine your own groins like puckish chimps. So:

115

Dear me,
Can an omnipotent god create a rock he can't pick up?
Adrian, London

This question has kept monks, hermits, and men in scratchy shirts who don't get out enough puzzling for well over 1,000 years. It is a question with a built-in trapdoor. So what do you think? Don't stress yourself. Both answers are wrong. Or not right. When a reasonable question has no reasonable answer it usually means it's the wrong question. So you should reword it. Why would God want to make a rock he can't pick up? To settle a dare? A bet? To impress the guys down the Vatican? What you should question is the word "omnipotent". Just say it a couple of times. It's a very . . . erect word. A very . . . assertive word. A can-do word. A superhero word. It's a blokey word. And it's too small, too limiting for God. The question should be: could a perfect god make a rock he couldn't pick up? Now the answer is far easier. The more theologically pressing question is: could a perfect god do something evil? The Old Testament is full of acts that look spiteful, occasionally wicked and they are either directly caused or condoned by God. Isn't the vengeance of a vengeful god itself an imperfection? These are not easy questions. But they should keep you away from

116

"which manbag should I wear?" Incidentally, the answer to that is: neither. Any sartorial journey that ends up at the crossroads of "which manbag?" is using the wrong fucking fashion sat-nav.

Dear me,
What has led to the greatest improvement in a chap's life over
the last 500 years?

Adrian, London

OK, form an orderly queue. Plainly: antiseptic, antibiotics, anaesthetics, indoor plumbing, the kettle, trades unions, motorcars, aeroplanes, trains, bicycles (the greatest of these, internationally, is the bicycle), the international rule of law, the international rules of association football, the internet, the moving camera, white bread, the chip . . . They're all contenders. Each in a grand or precise way has improved the lot of men. And we could throw in the safety razor, lucky underpants and amateur pornography. But it's ideas that really change the world we live in. Penicillin and plastic bags help a lot, fridges and hot water make manliness more comfortable and Tom Ford's fragrance range makes it smell better, but the idea that has pushed our lives into the light more than any other -ism or -ology is feminism. Oi! Sit down. I'm not finished. This is important. Because you need to man up and recognise how many of the good things you take for granted, how much of the mayo in the sandwich of your life is down to women's liberation. And we're not talking about the liberation to make lesbian porn or neck alcopops. It's not the liberation of pole dancing and pubic alopecia. The women's movement has given you half the human race as a present, as equals and friends. And nothing has been bigger than that. Liberation combined with contraception was a really big deal for everyone's sex life. Actually, it invented the sex life. But the great winners of the women's movement weren't women. It gave them a great fury at the scale of the injustice of the past and the distance yet to cover. The trouble with righting some wrongs is that it makes the remaining ones seem even more unbearable. But it's you lot who were the real beneficiaries of the movement. You did precious little to help. You sat on the sofa with your hand down your pants and sneered while at every step forward, women made your life better. And it cost you nothing. But it gave you a better mum, better sisters, better people to work with, to drink with, to tell you jokes, to go on holiday with and just to hang out with. Think of your last weekend session in the pub. Now imagine it without girls.

Dear Uncle Dysfunctional,
What shall I wear in bed?

Sam, Hastings

Sam, I can't tell whether you're a boy or a girl. Is that another problem we're not talking about? And you don't say if you're sleeping on your own or with another boy or another girl or a rough-haired terrier. My grandmother, bless her heart (she is, as we speak, sleeping in what's left of a plywood mahogany-effect coffin under a tonne of clay), always said that you should go to bed in the expectation that you may be woken up by a fireman. In her case, it was more wishful thinking than fearful. She always wore a wool nightie, a shawl, what they used to call an opera cardigan and knee-length bed socks, finished off with a hat. What she imagined this was going to do for the fireman I can't begin to think, but as a small child I found it terrifying. She looked exactly like the wolf who'd eaten my grandmother. That doesn't really answer your question, does it?

You see, it all depends on what you want to happen in bed. If you expect it to be the best bit of the day then, like Marilyn Monroe, you should perhaps wear just two drops of French perfume. And that goes for both sexes – everybody should go to bed smelling nice. In fact, everybody should

120

wake up smelling nice. I go further, there is not an excuse, ever, not to smell nice, particularly your feet. And your bedroom shouldn't smell like a Romanian STD clinic. Sorry, back to what you wear in bed. It's all about intent and being appropriate for the job in hand. The very worst thing to find in bed is someone wearing pants. Nothing is more terminally prophylactic than pants in bed. They are either the ones you've been wearing all day, which doesn't bear thinking about, or they're the special ones you put on for lying down in. People who have dedicated horizontal under-wear either don't fancy you, or anyone else, or have incontinent effluvial issues. Either way, you're not going there. And men who wear a combination of sports kit and underwear to go to bed in – which I see is so popular on soap operas and dramas about people who murder strangers – are again an unpleasant mixed message. Why would you want to sleep with someone who looks like they're preparing to work out?

So it should be all or nothing. If it's not nothing then it should be pyjamas or a nightdress, and they should never be ostentatiously erotic – it just looks like you're trying too hard. And by the time you've got into bed all the due diligence has already been done. This is just the packaging your present comes in. I was trying to remember what the worst things I'd ever seen in bed were, and once I had a girl who couldn't sleep unless she was wearing her father's long johns. And then there was one who wore a mink eyeshield: she said it was not to block out the light, just so that she couldn't see me. She said I wasn't to be offended, she just couldn't see anybody while she was having sex because it was confusing. And there have been various raggies and blankies and noonoos and awful bits of cloth, which come with the consistency of mummies' bandages.

I did have a girlfriend who was a bunny girl and she would come to bed in her ears, which I rather liked. I heard of a girl who could only have sex with men wearing rubber gloves (them, not her). And I know a man who took a first date to bed and discovered that she was wearing a strap-on penis – and then discovered that she wasn't.

Dear Unc Dysfunc,

A girl I've been sort of mucking about with said she couldn't love anyone who didn't love The Bell Jar. *Apparently, this* Bell Jar *isn't anything to do with kitchen equipment. It's a book by some other bitch. So, I said I couldn't love anyone who didn't love* Grand Theft Auto V *and then we had a row and now she's going with some nonce who wears a scarf indoors. What's all that about? I've mentioned this to some mates and they've noticed the same thing. Not* The Bell Jar, *but other stuff. One girl said she couldn't love anyone that didn't love* Anna Karenina. *So, my mate said he'd never touched her but if she was fit and wanted a threesome he was up for it. And then there's this gang of girls down the pedestrian precinct who are always mocking me and my mates, shouting, "You never read no Jane Austen, mong boy!" This has just happened in the last year or so. What's going on? I need a list of books that I can say I've read, that will get me loved. Just give me a heads up. You get me, bruv?*

Piers, by email

It's hell out there, Piers. It's a fucking library. It's this thing that happens to girls. They come over all fictional. It gets really bad in their late teens. They're generally over it by the time they're 30 but I doubt you want to wait that long. There's no point in trying to cheat on books. You'll just get caught out. And if there's one thing worse than being an illiterate philistine it's being an insecure illiterate philistine. And don't google "philistine", it looks needy. Leave literature to the birds. No threesome ever conceived is worth having to plough through *Little Women* for. (That's a novel, not dwarf sex.)

What I suggest is that you up the cultural stakes. Get poetry. Then you say, "Oh, you must know Keats' 'Ode on Melancholy'? Come back to mine and I'll read it to your twat." Nothing beats poetry. It's the death star of culture. It's the bollocks. And most of all, it's short and rhymes. And if you don't understand it, that's OK because you're supposed to just feel it, like Deep Heat. And you'd be surprised by how much you already know. Songs are all poetry, and they don't make any sense. I tell you, once a girl's got a dose of novels she's a pushover for iambic pentameter. They've got no literary immune system. Sonnets are like aural Viagra, so don't go quoting to people you don't want to get with. "*Though seen of none save him whose strenuous tongue / Can burst Joy's grape against his palate fine / His soul shalt taste the sadness of her might . . .*" Fuck knows what that means but it's the best hook-up line in the world.

AA,

My girlfriend says she'd like me to be more assertive in bed. So,
I said, tell me what you want and I'll do my best. She just rolled
her eyes and muttered, "Typical."

Norman, Cheltenham

Norman, we've had a number of letters along this line: "My
partner says she wants to feel she's being rogered, not
directing an interior decorator"; "I've done my best to be
a caring sympathetic and sensitive lover but my wife has
just told me she's bored to tears with my bedroom good
manners and relentless consideration. She'd like me to be
a bit more selfish and demanding. Do you think she needs
to see a counsellor? Yours, Giles." All of you: sex isn't fair.
It's never going to be fair. It's not an equal opportunity. It's
not even explicable. Sometimes, though, it seems that God
or Darwin – whichever came first – hardwired the wrong
sort of instructions into the wrong bodies. Men would be
much happier if girls behaved like men and women would
prefer it if men were as imaginative as women. There is a
problem. It's boredom. Women get bored with sex far
quicker than men. In fact, no man has ever become bored
with sex. We like familiarity, we perform better when there's
no anxiety, no unforeseen distractions. Women on the other

hand, well on both hands actually, think that familiarity is overfamiliar, that comfort is overrated. They need excitement and surprises and suspense. Sex is like shoes. Men like their shoes to be comfortable. Women like their shoes to be new. You see the problem here. When she said she wanted you to be more dominant, what she meant is: do something out of character, don't ask my permission, stop pussyfooting, stop saying please and thank you. Now, a sex expert would say – by the way, no one is a sex expert, anyone who tells you they're a sex expert is compensating for being a lousy shag, can you imagine hopping on board a self-defined sex expert? – anyway, what they would say is: role play. It's what they say about everything. It's the easiest way to make over your sex life: pretend it's someone else's sex life. You be the burglar, I'll be the quadriplegic in the wheelchair with the head wand and the number of the safe. You be Helen of Troy, I'll be the wooden horse. You be Jar Jar Binks, I'll be Margaret Thatcher. The possibilities are endless: a sort of hideous, karaoke, trick-or-treat sex life.

I don't know about you, but I find being myself with no clothes on quite difficult, so having to be Genghis Khan or a Dambuster would be too hideously, shrivellingly humiliating. There is another option: rope and gaffer tape. Bondage and sadomasochism are quite complicated (don't try them when not at home). There's an awful lot of knots to remember. Quite a bit of engineering to take into account. And you've got to constantly be aware that it's still sex, not hostage negotiation or cookery. You need to be very confident for sadism. You've got to keep the atmosphere electric. One wrong move, one slipknot, one Velcro cuff on the pubic hair and it can all descend into Norman Wisdom chaos. But there is a third way. If I was going to write a sex manual, it would be only one page with one word. And that word would be: blindfold. Dangerous and erotic without ever needing to put on a funny hat or an accent, a blindfold does it all for you. Immediately, it makes you dominant, adds suspense, excitement and a heightened sensitivity. A blindfold is the most versatile and effective sex aid and, best of all, it makes you disappear. There's hours and hours of gibbering, panting fun to be had with a scarf and a clothes peg.

Dear Uncle Dysfunctional,

I have been successfully masturbating for at least six months (not continuously – that would be excessive, painful and inter-fere with my schoolwork). I understand that the ability to have sex and potentially father children comes with responsibilities, although I'm not planning on doing the latter imminently, while ardently hoping for some of the former. The weight of inferred adult manliness weighs heavily on my shoulders. I worry about how to be a man because I've got a load of penis in my hand but, in my head, I'm fantasising about Violet from The Incredibles *(she's been my ideal girl since forever). I'm an only child and I don't have a dad. Well, obviously, I must have a dad, but he's never bothered to introduce himself. I have a fantastic mum who's been a brilliant parent. We're not sad or lonely, or terribly under-privileged, but there isn't a male in my life I can talk to about this sort of thing. My granddad is a gent's outfitter and votes Ukip. His idea of being manly is polishing your shoes and knowing how to tie a Windsor knot. I have a lot of friends at school, but obviously I can't talk about this sort of thing to them. And teachers are all kidult low-achievers, who've been made emotionally dysfunctional by hanging around children too much. I really could do with a grown-up answer and, I suspect, so could a lot of your readers, who possibly aren't eloquent or evolved enough to ask the question straight out. Please, don't*

waste time telling me I'm precocious – I know, I've known for
years. That's how precocious I am.

Jamie, by email

Jamie, thank you for the update on your onanism. I know
you just want to share with absolutely everyone at the beginning, and you're right. But then I suspect you're always
right. This is an interesting and important question. Indeed,
in many ways, it is the question that everyone writes in
asking about. And I'll answer it as straightforwardly as I
can. You will grow up to be a man, whatever you do, whether
you think about it or not. It is what you are and most of
the things that make you a man are out of your control,
like erections, urges and smells, and the need to laugh at
things in groups that you wouldn't find remotely funny if
you were on your own. But what you mean is: how do you
become a good man? How do you mould and manipulate
that small portion of masculinity that isn't genes, hormones,
natural selection and hardwiring? The part that makes you
unique is the bit people will like or fear, fall in love with,
or try to avoid. Maybe it's best not to ask another man, a
failed or compromised manly man. Maybe the best person
would be a woman. She might tell you what was attractive
and most endearing from her point of view.

I suspect women would say you should be sensitive but
capable, strong but also flexible, and that you should be able
to change a tyre and have an argument without shouting.
You should be dependable but spontaneous, clean and dirty.
The ideal man for a woman, in short, might be a handyman
butler with benefits. On the other hand, the male exemplar

of manliness is Shane, the hero of a 1953 cowboy film you haven't seen, a sort of Arthurian knight – tough, honourable, caring and just. And that's fine for everyone else, but it's the most uncomfortable and miserable person to actually be in real life. It's lonely, tortured and hard, and is not any use going round a supermarket. Trying to learn to be a good man is like learning to play tennis against a wall. You are only a good man – a competent, capable, interesting and lovable man – when you're doing it for, or with, other people. So, being a good man is not an exam or a qualification, it changes, and it incorporates being a good friend, a good father, a good employee, a good boss, a good neighbour and a good citizen. The end of a rather long answer is: there is no short answer. But I can tell you a few things: learn to apologise, say sorry often and with absolute conviction, and without caveat; for women, there is no such thing as good-natured teasing, it is all mockery and is an irreversible passion-killer; humour isn't as important as people say it is, being made to laugh is nice because it's inclusive, cosy and unthreatening but what you laugh at isn't really that important. Learning Jimmy Carr riffs off by heart is not the way to anyone's heart, unless you're Jimmy Carr. And remember, the two most attractive things in a man are a sense of danger and being able to make a girl feel really safe. The definition of a good man is perhaps a chap who can do both those things simultaneously, so good luck.

❖ ❖ ❖

Dear Uncle Dysfunctional,
I really want to try anal. How shall I bring it up with my new
girlfriend?

Miles, Brighton

Simple, dude. Just ask her to strap on a dildo and whack it up your bum.

Dear Uncle Dysfunctional,

What age is too old to wear a leather jacket? I've always really fancied a sort of American flying jacket thing – a bit Top Gun, *you know – but I've never been able to afford one before. And now I can, my wife says I'm too old. This seems terribly unfair and, actually, I mind more than I should as it would have been the fulfilment of a childhood dream and now, whatever I do, she's spoilt it for me. I'm not going to tell you my age, I just want your final judgement and I will abide by that.*

Ralph, Birmingham

OK, Ralph. The rule is, you can't wear things with a practical application after the age you would realistically be expected to perform the job they're designed for. So flying jackets are pretty much off your radar after 30. Sheepskin, of course – the uniform of second division football managers – you can wear right up into your sixties but not if you're 20. Donkey jackets only if you're fit enough to carry a hod, and no one should be a navvy after 25. Pea coats: if you're too old to join the Marines, don't think about it. Cowboy boots you can't wear unless you actually are a cowboy or in a Status Quo tribute band, or over 60; there's something about a retiring gent in cowboy boots that looks sort of presidential.

So much of life is not about whether you're good or bad, or right or wrong, or can afford or not afford – it's just about timing. Wearing next season's look this season is as ridiculous as wearing last season's this season. There are five great ages of man – five moments when you need to reevaluate everything, clear out the cupboard and the wardrobe, and most importantly, your head. They are 13, 20, 30, 40 and 60. All men need to know this.

13

Thirteen is perhaps the biggest one – it's the end of childhood and the beginning of being a teenager. You get balls and can't sing "O for the wings of a dove" any more. Things you are already too old for at 13 include birthday parties with clowns, Nerf guns, a 10-second start, the light on, Valentine's cards from your nan, having your mum wash any of your body parts. But you can start swearing as part of normal sentence structure (and not just stand-alone expletives), and wearing T-shirts that have pictures or slogans that refer to contemporary music. You can do weird adolescent shit with your hair, you can offer your seat on the bus to an older person, and you can kill things – rabbits, fish, nits. And, of course, there are the three big ones: you can wank, drink and smoke.

20

Twenty is a tough age because it slips past in the middle of so much else – university, gap year, leaving home, getting jobs. The big birthdays are still perceived to be 18 and 21, but 20 is where you need to have a programme, to have a pogrom, make a bonfire of your previous life. So, 20 is the age where you finally, irrevocably put childish things behind you. "I forgot" is no longer an excuse, neither is "I overslept", or "If you rinse them out, you can use them again." Neither is wearing the same T-shirt or underpants for a week, or odd socks. At 20, you need to have a pair of leather shoes with laces, and a suit. At 20, you can't be sick in the street, or in someone else's Wellington boots. Twenty is too old to dump a girl simply because you want to go to a festival in Serbia. It's too old to shoplift or do wheelies on a pushbike. It's too old to run down the street with a pretend assault rifle, and it's too old to sing Whitney Houston songs at the back of a bus at midnight. But it's not old enough to marry, be a father or give up on learning stuff. Or to decide you're not good at anything. Twenty is the age when you start moving the intellectual furniture into the cerebral emotional house you've been building since you were two. At 20, you should be able to cook proper food, not just fried, stoned, dude-munchies. Oh, and no more tattoos. But also remember you're never too old to fold a paper aeroplane and fly it while making the noise of the Spitfire's mighty Merlin engine soaring over the South Downs on a perfect June day.

30

Thirty is the man-up year. You stop smoking and doing coke. Now, you really are too old to wear a T-shirt anywhere but in the gym, and you should be there for health, not beauty. You can't do hoodies any more, or trainers. No, really – no trainers. You should be able to tie a bow tie, have shirts that need cufflinks, and you can't play kick-about football with the other balding, paunchy blokes on Wednesday evening. You all look pathetic. Thirty is the age when you have to admit that you will never play any professional sport, you will never be needed for a national team, and you can't wear shorts in the city, or Speedos on the beach. From now on, your life is intellectual rather than physical, so you need to polish up your lounge act. At 30, you should have made at least one speech in public without using notes or nicking a joke off the internet. At 30, you shouldn't eat and sleep in the same room. You should be in a relationship that shares more than bodily fluids. At 30, when people ask, you should be able to say what you are rather than what you hope to be. At 30, you should already know what your favourite novel is – and it shouldn't be *Harry Potter*. And neither should that be your favourite film. You should own all the formal clothes you will ever need, and at 30 you should have taken your parents out to dinner.

40

Everyone knows that 40 is crunch time. Forty is the age you dread. Over 40, there is a dreadful, grey, terminal prognosis. It seems to be the pivot on the seesaw of life. Before 40, everything is acquisition; after 40, it's all conservation. Actually, 40 is the age where you need to have a moratorium on making big decisions; don't buy anything that costs more than £1,000, and don't get rid of anything worth more than £1,000. The best way to avoid a midlife crisis is to not buy one. Don't grow your hair or a beard; don't drive a car with a detachable roof. And no one at 40, except a policeman, should be seen on a motorbike, particularly a Harley-

Davidson. Riding a Harley-Davidson should be a punishment, like community service or being put in the stocks. Forty is when experience should count for more than enthusiasm. By 40, you should have travelled to at least four continents. You should have made a success of a career, not just a job. Forty is when you check yourself for all the signs of being a kidult. So, no more jeans. Ever.

60

Sixty is harvest festival – this is where you pick up the fruit of your life. This is the age where you start smoking again, and doing recreational drugs. When you're 60, you can sing anything you damn well like at the back of a bus. And the best thing about dressing up at 60 is that you can start wearing other people's national costume: djellabas, kurtas, Austrian boiled wool, Sami hats. Sixty is the first age where it's not just acceptable but admirable to have a girlfriend half your age. Sixty is when you can offer opinions whether people want them or not. At 60, you can play with soldiers and Lego again, have naps in the afternoon and run down the high street with an imitation assault rifle. You can wear Speedos again because, frankly, who cares? At 60, you should be witty rather than funny, and you will know the importance of detail. The only thing you can't wear at 60 is a look of censorious disappointment.

Dear Uncle Dysfunctional,

You never answer the problems of people with unusual, or as I like to call them bespoke, sexual needs; what the ignorant call perverted. Why does some dull hetero who just wants to shag his nanny need advice? "Don't do it, vanilla dick," should suffice. Ninety per cent of the world is sexually bland, libidinous Lego. Nine per cent is gay. One per cent is imaginative. It's me. We have needs that are not found in the convenience store of eroticism. We are not boil-in-the-bag or off-the-peg, although sometimes you may find us astride the peg. And we could use a bit of advice. Not least how to cope with the slow and painful realisation that we are different. That we will only find erotic fulfilment and a blessed relief from frustration if a fat lass eats marzipan and then shits on our chest. Or, finally find someone who will treat us like a baby. Or, in my personal case, a muscular woman in sensible shoes who will abuse me. For the rest of you, breaking up with your spotty, awkward, sexually repressed girlfriend is no more than an inconvenience. You could conceivably get off with most of the people on the next bus that comes along. I have to find a needle in a haystack. (As a masochist, I'm always searching haystacks for needles.) Most of us exotics lead lives of frustrated loneliness punctuated, if we're lucky, with occasional humiliations we have to pay someone to fulfil. But generally, we are reduced to solitary acts of gratification. For a

moment, try to imagine the complications of having even a
simple wank if you are a committed masochist. It doesn't bear
thinking about, except thinking about misery is one of the few
little pleasures I get. Can you offer any solace?

Bill, by email

Don't beat yourself up, Bill.

Mr Gill,

You know, they talk about girls who can't say no and how they're slappers and the like. Well, I envy them. I was brought up very strictly by my mother after my father left us. We were very poor and life was very hard. She hated all men and drummed it into me that I was not to give them anything and not to do anything that might encourage them. Girls who attracted men "were no better than they should be". Now I'm 20 and my mum's in an old people's home. I'm pretty. I've got a good figure. Athletic. I've got a nice job and my own flat. And plenty of friends. But I still can't say yes. When it comes to second dates, or coming back to mine for coffee, or even another drink, I always say no, even if on the inside I'm screaming yes, yes, yes. I keep hearing my mother's voice and what comes out is no, no, no. It's ruining my life. Please, please, please can you help?

Caitlin, by email

No.

Dear Uncle Dysfunctional,

What the fuck is a fucking man bag? What is a man supposed to fucking put in his fucking man bag? Why does my previously normal fucking girlfriend want me to get a fucking man bag, and is she now showing me fucking bags for men that cost a fucking grand in change? What the fuck is that about? Around here, the things you keep in a man bag are your bollocks.

Neil, Basingstoke

Whoa. Calm down, Neil. Let's start with the name. The problem with a man bag is that it's called a man bag. "Man bag" is obviously unconscionable. You can't go into a pub and say, "Sorry, has anyone seen my man bag?" or, "Nice man bag you've got there, mate. Is it Gucci?" OK. So what if you call it carry-on luggage? See, already your fists are unclenched, you're breathing through your nose again – carry-on luggage is fine. You're cool with carry-on. Maybe even urban rucksack, messenger bag. That's rugged. So we're over the "over my dead body" thing, but the question mark still hangs over the content: what do you put in a man bag? An iPad, possibly. If you look at what women carry in their handbags, it's a revelation. And a warning. First, always ask before going through a lady's handbag, even if they're really close by and you bought the bag; handbags

140

are intimate and deeply personal. There is a whole feminist inquiry that questions the symbolism of handbags and we don't need to go there. Suffice it to say, you wouldn't shove your hands down a girl's knickers without asking; the same goes for handbags. Women's handbags are incredibly heavy. You rarely get to pick one up and, when you do, you wonder why anyone carries so much stuff around all day. And if you did tip one out onto a table, you'd see that 90 per cent of the contents is rubbish: odd bits of gunk and stubs of splat that are never going to be useful, bits of food, sweets, chocolate, books, enormous amounts of loose change. Have you noticed that almost all the change in the world goes to women? When was the last time you had a five pence piece? Exactly. In a Christmas pudding. All the rest of it is in women's handbags. They also carry a phenomenal amount of shit that pertains to hair: brushes, sprays, clips, grips, bands, ribbons. When you look through a woman's handbag, you realise that the bag itself is demanding to be filled. "Feed me," it says, "feed me." As handbags get ever more absurdly large, so they need to carry more stuff to validate the expense of this huge trunk with chains, buckles and padlocks on. Men on the other hand have spent a generation trying to get rid of stuff – we dumped the briefcase two decades ago. Carrying shit is a sign that you're a drone, a runner. It's the work experience who carries things. Most of us are down to keys, a phone and a card. That's it. Get a man bag and it'll start whispering to you – "feed me, feed me" – and the next thing, you'll be thinking about getting a Filofax. I've made a random list of things that men used to carry in their pockets and now don't:

handkerchiefs, matches, cigarettes, a pipe, pipe tobacco, pipe cleaners, wallet, a cheque book, a penknife, an address book, a diary, an *A–Z*, a spectacle case (glasses used to be made of glass), a fountain pen. Men were walking man bags. Suits hung like elephants' arses. No, as you were, Neil – resist the man bag. Carry-on luggage if you're flying, a tote bag if you're on the beach, messenger bag if you're on a bike, rucksack if you're hiking. For everyday, all you need is a phone, a card and a smile. Incidentally, an old gent's put-down used to be, "He looks like the sort of chap who carries keys." You see, a gentleman of worth always had someone to open all his doors for him.

Dear Uncle Dysfunctional,
Apparently, 55 per cent of married Frenchmen have affairs.
That is an incredible figure. Really, more than half are cheating
on their wives. How can they call themselves a civilised and
moral country? How could you possibly trust a Frenchman
about anything? You know, I thought I was pretty broad-minded
but I'm disgusted. What do you have to say about that?

Nigel, Herne Bay

What I find most shocking about that is that 45 per cent
of Frenchmen are lying – to everyone, not just their wives.

Dear Uncle Dysfunctional,

I was driving to work. It was the rush hour. I was late. I left my husband eating muesli and listening to the breakfast show on Good Morning Bristol, in his dressing gown. I was on the one-way bit in the town centre, where there's a tricky filter by the bus station when the car died – just stopped. Didn't even cough. Just stopped. Nothing. Right in the middle of the road. In the rush hour. Everyone was honking and shouting, so I got out and ran home. I just ran home. As I opened the door and went into the kitchen, there was my husband, dressed in a girl's school uniform with a clip-on ponytail, giving oral sex to a very fat Chinese man. Actually, a Malaysian of Chinese descent, I found out later. He was very upset – my husband, not the Malaysian – he said he'd never done this before and it was an aberration, and perhaps he was depressed, or there was something in the muesli, and he'd get help. I must say, I found that difficult to believe. You don't just stumble upon a schoolgirl's uniform and think, "I wonder if it fits." And then, "Oh my, it does fit. And now I have an overwhelming desire to fellate an obese Oriental." Apparently, it was the first time he'd done it in the kitchen. Normally he uses the garage or the spare bedroom, but the Chinaman-slash-Malaysian was peckish, and wanted some toast and Nutella whilst having his willy licked. And that's when I lost it. "We haven't got any Nutella," I exclaimed. "It's on my list." At this point, my husband said he was going to kill himself and locked himself in the cupboard under the stairs. The Chinese-slash-Malaysian man said I owed him 50 quid, and if it wasn't Nutella, then what was on his toast. Please, can you help?

Stella, there are a number of reasons a car could just stop like that. First thing: did you check there was petrol in the tank? You might have just run out. You didn't mention if it's an automatic or a manual. I'm assuming it's automatic, in which case it's probably an electrical fault, possibly a blown fuse. The fuse box is most likely in the glove compartment. Did you try to take the key out and then put it in again? Sometimes it just needs to restart. If none of these worked, you're best to call one of the roadside assistance services. If you don't know if you're already a member, you can check with your insurer. Often, membership comes with your policy. By the way, what was on the toast?

Dear Uncle Dysfunctional,

I'm in my first year at uni, studying medicine. I want to specialise in neurosurgery. My dad was a miner, now he's on disability. And my mum is a cleaner and a local councillor. I'm their only child and we're a very close family. I love them both immensely, and would never do anything to hurt them. Obviously, there was no spare cash to send me to college and I really didn't want to be lumbered with a huge debt, so I've got a part-time job that works out quite nicely. The thing is, how can I tell them I'm a stripper? Well, more of a lap-dancer, actually. They were so proud when I got into university. Every time my dad tried to tell one of his mates, he'd start crying. The work's not bad. The customers are ghastly, of course, but the other girls are lovely. Most of them are studying something; we've got three physicists, a couple of PPEs and a philosopher with the best tits you've ever seen.

Julie, Manchester

My first thought, Julie, is: don't. Why would you tell them? Why is it so important that they know? There are lots and lots of things you didn't tell them because it would upset them. You didn't come down to breakfast and say, "Wow, I just lost my anal virginity. I don't know what all the fuss was about." Or, "I got a lift last night from Ted, who was so out of it on vodka and acid, I had to steer." I suppose there is a chance that they might find out by accident – one of your dad's mates might come in, or one of the punters might murder you. But as a doctor, of course, you're going to have to learn to lie to people all the time. You're going to sit in consulting rooms and look sincerely into their terrified trusting eyes, and say that everything is going to be fine, and of course they'll be well enough to go to their granddaughter's wedding. Or that the little lad will be back on his bike in no time, when you know that they're going to be spares and smoke in a couple of months. Get used to it. You will learn that telling them the truth is not the same as giving them all the facts. The truth for your parents is that they brought up a clever, conscientious girl who's going to be a doctor. The fact that dozens of convenience-store owners and scaffolders are staring up her gaping clam's pocket while making obscene slurping noises, doesn't change a thing. Not much. Not really.

Dear Uncle Dysfunctional,
Do you think that using a prostitute should be made illegal?
                                                      Alex, Stoke Newington

This is just another of our deeply weird civic relationships
with other people's bits. It would then be legal to sell sex
but not buy it. Do you think we might do that with drugs?
Or guns? Why is selling sex different from selling your love
and nurturing instincts by being a nanny? The worst thing
about prostitution is the lack of respect and opprobrium,
and the pity and the assumptions that are piled onto prostitutes. If you're now shouting, "What about trafficking?
What about the violence? And what about pimping?" Well,
they are already illegal. Whatever the trade, it's a crime –
trafficking brussels sprout pickers is illegal. And hurting
anyone is plainly illegal. Pimps aren't exempt from complying
with health and safety, and employment law. The root cause
of all the dangers and miseries of prostitution is that society
despises prostitutes and the men who use them. So I wouldn't
make any of it illegal. What I would do is insist that anyone
who used a prostitute had to work as a prostitute once a
year, just to see what it was like. There should be an annual
"Take Your Punter to Work" day. Men who've bought sex
will have to sell sex: a hand job, perhaps, an assisted shower,

perhaps pissing on a stressed farmer, turning up to a foot-ballers' spit roast. The answer to all of society's prurience, embarrassment and censoriousness is not less sex, it's more sex. Not publicly managed and approved sex, but freedom from collective judgement about who you do it with, how often you have it and who you have it with. Also, how you charge for it: whether you take cash upfront or wait till after the wedding; whether you exchange it for housekeeping, protection and mutual vanity, or for a standing order. Anyone who thinks that all sex that isn't philanthropic or altruistic should be criminalised has no sense of biology or economics. There is also something to be said about making everyone file audited sexual accounts each year, which we could all then go and look up at Companies House.

Dear Uncle Dysfunctional,

I found a copy of Esquire *in my son's room, 10 minutes after I found him in bed with a friend's daughter. And 10 minutes after that I read your "advice column". Inverted commas are surely not big enough to attach to these words. Such a pity the keyboard doesn't have a key for clothes pegs or rubber gloves. "Ho ho," you may think. "Typical mum, didn't knock first." No, I didn't knock. This is my own house and I don't knock on doors in my own house. And anyway, this was 2.30 in the afternoon and I assumed that he'd be out. And, at the risk of titillating your jaded and morally dull palate, I'm going to tell you what I found: not teenagers covertly exploring the joyful possibilities of their budding bodies, but a girl on all fours, having her back door kicked in. Oh yes, I know all the lingo, Mr Gill. I wasn't born yesterday and I'm no prude. There was a chemical smell in the room, which I remembered was amyl nitrate. What shocked me – and I'm still shocked – was the obvious casual sophistication of their sex: it looked like they were acting out pornography, and it has depressed me to tears. How can we have allowed our children's innocence and their sense of excitement and discovery at the unfolding pleasure and agony of a sex life that will have to sustain them throughout their lives to be poisoned by the vile body of sewage of online porn? It's not that it's immoral (though, of course, it is) or exploitative and misogynistic (which it also is), it's that it's so pathetically fifth-rate as sex, so dull and mechanical, so banal and boring. Oh, I don't expect you to understand or agree, but just in the hope that there's a twinge of unsullied responsibility under all that cynicism – especially as an old man with children – I'd like to hear whatever it is that you have to say. Incidentally, my son is 16 and the friend's daughter is 18.*

Phillipa, via email

Obviously, Phillipa, you and probably most of the readers will expect me to issue an answer with a "woo woo – respect for your boy" and print a lot of fist-pumping emoticons. Are there fist-pumping emoticons? But I'm not going to. What looked like a porn mime to you was a fraught and heart-pounding construction of performance anxiety, pimple anxiety, smelly-breath anxiety, inexperience anxiety, spiced with hope, lust, excitement. And then, just as he was hanging out the back of some older, more sophisticated, cooler bird, his mother walks in. For God's sake: let's start with what's really damaging here. Let's separate reality from virtual and fantasy. You not giving your son any privacy is what's really wrong here, and you know you're in the wrong because you started off with a lot of self-justifying bluster about not knocking on doors in your own house, as if ownership relegates everyone else's right to privacy. And you would certainly have knocked if it had been your elderly aunt with her new Algerian boyfriend in there. So, the first thing is, you owe your boy a big and abject apology, and a promise that you'll never, ever walk in on him unannounced again. Just pray that you haven't made him impotent or a premature ejaculator for life, and that you don't need to start saving for 15 years of Freudian analysis. Now, the second, less important bit of your letter: porn on the internet. And I do have some sympathy with you. I can't watch it any more. I'm old and I suffer from empathy. I can't look at people copulating and not think, "Oh Lord, she must be about the same age as my daughter. And she must be someone else's daughter. And one day, she'll be a mother. And he'll go for a promotion in his bank. And this image will come up in the search his employers do on his past." So, let's start by agreeing that the people most at risk from pornography are those who are in it, who make it, and I say that as someone who has made a porn movie themselves, using my real name. (Still available somewhere out there on the net, *Hot House Tales*. It's got Ron Jeremy in it. Fill your boots – he can.) You and I both worry about every 13-year-old having seen everything that is humanly possible, and a lot of things that really aren't. And that's because we grew up without computers and our grandparents thought much the same about television ruining us. We worry about this because we worry about sex. Sex was always secret and private, and, let's face it, dirty and shameful. When we look at porn on the net, we can only see it in terms of our learned attitudes to sex. I don't know anyone of my generation who can't tell the difference between real life and television. And anyone old enough to have consensual sex will be astonished at how unlike porn real sex actually is. I don't believe teenagers are that different from us, or our grandparents, or our great-grandparents. I just know that every generation thinks that the next generation is going to purgatory by way of anal sex, which, incidentally, isn't innately rude or dirty or evil or humiliating, it's the preferred position for at least 10 per cent of the male population, including Oscar Wilde, Alan Turing and Leonardo da Vinci. If this generation grows up a little less ignorant and fearful than we were, then that's all to the good. And if internet porn helps, then that's a positive. Probably not an excuse but a mitigation. In the end, sex is complicated and brilliant, with layers of emotional baggage, none of which porn has. What's surprising is not how graphically specific pornography is, or has become, but how very unlike the experience of sex it remains.

Dear Uncle Dysfunctional,

My girlfriend wants me to wear a T-shirt that says, "This is what a feminist looks like," and Facebook, Twitter and Instagram it. And I feel uncomfortable about it. It's not that I disagree with the politics, I'm just not what a feminist looks like. I'm what a 24-year-old Nigerian graphic designer who spends too much time in the gym looks like. She says that it's cool and it would reflect well on her and, anyway, what's the big deal? Don't I want to support her and don't I think that women's suffrage is worth wearing a T-shirt for, and I expect her to cook and wash my boxers and suck my cock like some Victorian indentured maid, and all she's asking is that I support her and other women, not least my sister and mother, and possibly our daughter, if she ever decides to have sex with me again, by wearing a fucking T-shirt for two minutes? And what's the point of spending all that time in the gym if I can't wear a T-shirt for the girls? And then she said, you know, as a black man, I should identify with the struggle. And then, I admit, I lost it a bit and said, "Really? You wear a T-shirt that says 'black is beautiful' and hope that people don't think you are some fantasist beeyatch", and that's when it started to get really nasty. So what do you think, Unc?

John, Alderley Edge

OK, John. I asked my daughter whether a man could be a feminist, and she got quite angry. "Daddy, how long have you been my father? And you still have to ask that. Of course you can be a feminist. You should be a feminist. And if you're not a feminist, I'm not going to take any more allowance off you. What you can't be is a woman – you don't know what it's like to be a woman so you can't share the pain, the humiliation, the fear, the fucking rage, but you can be on our side without being a sad, pussy-whipped wanker because you want the best for me, and you are proud of what I achieve. And if anyone paid me less than the other waiter, you'd come and close their restaurant down."

"You're not a waiter. You'd make a terrible waiter. You'd tell people 'not to have that' and not to look at their phones while eating."

"That's not the point, Dad. The point is you are a feminist because you have a daughter who's a feminist, and I am not going to have a paternalistic father."

"Well, hold on . . ."

"Don't correct my grammar. You know what I mean. So write back and tell the doofus not to wear the T-shirt."

"Really, I thought you were going to say he should wear the T-shirt."

"Of course not. Political and social justice is one thing; reducing them to selfies is pathetic. Reducing what Emily Davison did, what the force-fed suffragettes did, what Andrea Dworkin and Germaine Greer wrote, to a fucking silly slogan on a T-shirt, is hideous and counterproductive. And, anyway, the whole semiology of T-shirts is bad: Third

155

World sweatshops; wet T-shirt competitions; pressure on women to be skinny and look sexy for men. No. Equal pay, representation and safety on the street is never going to be won by T-shirts, and the effort that this diverts detracts from the real, serious business of making the world equitable and fair."

"OK, so he shouldn't wear the T-shirt?"

"No, but he should cook her dinner, wash her knickers and suck her cock, and then let her roll over and go to sleep afterwards."

Dear Uncle Dysfunctional,

I know you've touched on this before but I think your answers have been flippant. I'm in real need of some serious advice – I'm desperate. I've never been this desperate before. I didn't know this could happen. I didn't know you could feel like this. I've never been so utterly, utterly hopelessly unhappy. I don't know what to do. I've always known what to do: I'm very capable and optimistic and sensible and proactive and gregarious. I'm kind and realistic. And now I'm broken and helpless, and self-pitying, and mortally poleaxed by misery; reduced and incapacitated by pessimism. I can't bear company or people. I don't want friends. I can't talk, I can't think or plan or care about anything except my all-consuming sadness and loss. Sophie doesn't love me any more. She did; now she doesn't. I'm dumped, cast aside without hope of reprieve or reconciliation. She doesn't want to see me or talk to me until I no longer love her. Please, please.

Adam, via email

I've often thought that the one tangible clue that there might possibly be a God is the emotional Ebola of loving someone who no longer loves you. It is a feeling that is out of all proportion to almost every other human experience that doesn't involve a premature death. And there seems to be no particular Darwinian evolutionary reason for it. Why would we need to have this in our emotional repertoire? It can't be an aid to monogamy because the people who leave and fuck around don't get it. It is the punishment of the true, the innocent, the constant and the loving. Mind you, I don't know what's in it for God, either. I've been dumped by people I was utterly besotted with twice in my life. I don't know how I got through it but I read constantly, obsessively, like a 14-year-old girl with a slight frown and frizzy hair who had just discovered Jane Austen. But I only read funny books. In one case, all of Evelyn Waugh and, in the other, a great deal of PG Wodehouse. I'm not sure they did much more than mark time and keep me off parapets but, in retrospect, I think they had some solace in them. There is no cure for a broken heart. There is no secret, no training, no opiate for the soul, but the older I get, the more I believe in the emotional balm of art – books, music, painting. There is no convincing Darwinian explanation for creativity or genius, except that it can describe the internal tsunamis of the human condition. And in explaining, soothes, mitigates and finally uplifts. There is nothing anyone can say to you face-to-face that will make you feel better but, from a page or a stage or a canvas, they can. Why should we care about beauty at all? It serves little purpose, except as a gown and a bandage for love.

Dear Uncle Dysfunctional,

I like clothes, I like to look nice. I've a favourite jacket and a jumper I'm sentimental about, but they're just clothes. You know what I mean? In the end, they're only the wrapping the important stuff comes in. I don't want to spend a fortune on them. In fact, I don't want to spend anything. Buying shirts is so far down my bucket list of things to spend cash on, it doesn't register. I look smart, clean and comfortable. I'm cool in summer and warm in winter.

The thing is, my dad complains that I don't have the right clothes to visit my grandma or go to my cousin's wedding. And he had a fit when he saw me going for a job interview in the clothes that I wear to do everything else. I said that they only wanted me to talk on the phone, not to look like James Bond, but he wasn't having it. Why do you lot – old people – all insist on having a dressing-up box to do different shit in? A suit for drinking tea. A tie to meet a bank manager. It's weird. And, while we're at it, what's with all the clothes in men's magazines? Are there really blokes who look at the pages of stuff and think, "Ooh, I must spend my Saturday searching for just the right mid-length spring scarf in this season's must-have maroon"?

Dylan, via email

Yes, Dylan, there are. But let's step away from the absurdity of contemporary fashion, to strip your question down to its boxer shorts. When I was probably about your age, my dad – who actually thought very like you, hated wearing a tie and would have liked to have worn corduroy wherever possible all his life, and would much rather be warm than stylish – went to China, then still a closed communist country under Mao Zedong, coming to the end of the Cultural Revolution. He brought me back a Mao suit – blue cotton, a baggy safari jacket with four flat pockets, a ghillie collar, single-breasted, and chino trousers with a matching cap. It was the collective uniform of a billion Chinese of both sexes. It came in either blue for everyone or green for the military. And the answer to your question is yes, it was practical, cheap and it made everyone look the same on the outside and spared them the bourgeois worries of fashion, style, avarice and jealousy; they were never underdressed, always appropriate, it was a reminder that everyone is equal, and that what was important is what they did, said and thought.

I wore mine once, and cut quite a dash in Notting Hill Gate in the mid-Seventies. I looked like I was going to a fancy dress party, or playing in a movie. People pointed and laughed, and asked where I got it. Exactly the opposite of what Mao had wanted. It wasn't an expression of unity, but singularity, a statement of otherness. I never wore it again, choosing to look different in the same way as everyone else. But it was an irony with a lesson in the power of what you dismissively call fashion and I pretentiously call aesthetics. Personal adornment is the only cultural form that everybody in the world takes part in.

Even if you take the Clarkson line that if it covers your genitals, it's fine, that's a statement. Indeed, Jeremy opting out of fashion has made his look as recognisable and in-your-face as Grayson Perry's. You don't have a choice about fashion or aesthetics – you're in it, whether you like it or not. So you then have to decide, do you want to be good or naff at it? The truth about Mao's suits was that they didn't relieve you of the insecurity and vanity of surface things, calibrate the intellect and the character, they demanded that everyone had the same character and thought the same pocket platitudes. Removing variety in dress doesn't uncover variety of personality. The biggest, most avaricious, style-conscious fashion victims in the world are now the Chinese. So don't assume that you alone can rise above fashion. It really isn't a good look.

And as for the tiresomeness of having to dress differently for different situations, just get over it. You wouldn't like it if your mother had turned up at your graduation in her wedding dress, explaining that it had cost her so much she thought she should get it out more often, and if it was all right for one then why not for all special occasions? Of all the myriad and voluminous ways that a parent can embarrass their children, dress is the easiest and the most cripplingly effective. There are a very limited number of potential occasions where you should have the appropriate clothes:

– Obviously, you need a black tie: every man at some point in his life will have to wear black tie and, when choosing a suit, think, "Could my father or my grandfather wear this?" And if the answer is no, then you shouldn't either: black

161

tie should be ageless. And learn to tie a bow – it's not difficult and there's no excuse for either a clip-on or the hideous Hollywood straight tie. You do, though, need a straight black tie for funerals. Everyone has to go to a funeral at some time and you need to be dark and sombre, and in a black tie. Wearing a football scarf because he'd have appreciated it, or a Hawaiian shirt because he loved a laugh is not the point. Funerals are about respect for the bereaved, not a punch line for the dead.

– You need something smart that isn't a suit. That probably means a blazer, the most versatile piece of clothing ever invented.

– And you need a white shirt – not expensive, not fancy, just ironed. A white shirt is the ultimate result dress, the most seductive thing a man can wear. It's our equivalent of high heels and stockings. Every message a white shirt gives out is positive. It's unflashy but romantic.

– Advice to men about dressing tends to be formal but every man needs to have a good fancy dress. The rules are "wit rather than guffaws", "amusing is better than hilarious" – laughing with you, not at you. And nothing that's made out of polyester: you become a sweaty static-magnet. Nothing with a carnival head. And nothing you couldn't hail a taxi in at four in the morning.

– And a dressing gown, every man needs a good dressing gown. Not necessarily like Noël Coward but something that doesn't look like a DNA encyclopedia or evidence from a crime scene. Nothing above the knee, and nothing with dragons, eagles or Chinese writing on it. Oh, and not plucked from the Bangkok Four Seasons or a health club. It should be attractive enough for a date to wear it the next morning without gagging, laughing or regretting.

– Remember that clothes can never make you something you're not: they don't fool anyone but they do let people know who you think you are. Nature gave you your look and there's only a limited amount you can do about that, but what you wear is the skin you choose for yourself. More importantly than what it tells others, it reminds you of who you can be.

Dear Uncle Dysfunctional,

I've read that the "girl on top" position is the most likely to break a chap's willy. Who knew you could break a cock? And that getting your todger fractured is one of the most painful things to happen to a penis? Leaving aside the obvious humiliation of having it gawped at by masses of medical students and sniggering nurses who've never seen a bust one before, there's the awkward and equally painful operation that I understand is often unsuccessful and can lead to permanent erectile dysfunction and a willy like a small hockey stick, which is more use for unblocking sinks than being the wand of pleasure. And I expect it'll look weird in Speedos. I only ask because my boyfriend, well, my soon-to-be-ex-boyfriend, has been sticking his in all sorts of unsavoury places, and has given me a repellent and humiliating disease. And I'm considering giving him something to remember me by. So what do you suggest the best way to break his penis would be?

Deirdre, via email

An interesting question, Deirdre. And I'm not sure this is the best place to come to ask it. But you're quite right: "cowgirl", as it's known by porn stars and sex therapists, is the position most likely to result in a fractured willy. "Doggy" or "ewe" (if you're Welsh) is the second most winky wonky-damaging. However, it's rare, only accounting for one break in every gazillion knee-tremblers. So you, or rather he, is more likely to smash his sausage falling out of bed than actually slipping it up you. However, the most common cause for a bust penis is guilt and shame. In some Muslim countries, a visible erection is a terrible embarrassment and boys are taught how to detumesce in emergencies. I think this may be your best option in the disfigurement of the errant hard-on. I'm told that old mullahs suggest grabbing the base of the pee-pee in one fist while firmly grasping the bell end with the other, and sharply pulling it down at right angles. You should hear a distinct cracking noise, followed by a long, high-pitched scream. I would be remiss if I didn't point out, as an adviser on a men's magazine, that this is grievous bodily harm and could lead to a criminal prosecution. Also, a man with a broken knob is unlikely to be reasonable in his reactions. But I expect you've already thought about all that and might consider something a little less fundamental. The one thing worse than a broken cock is a broken heart. And worse than a broken heart is a crushed ego. So why don't you shag his dad, assigning the acid-piss crotch-rot that he gave to you to his parents? And then send them all a note on Facebook. Only a suggestion.

Dear AA,

Ricky has been my best mate since our first day at junior school. He was being bitten by another boy and crying like a cat in a kennel. So I thumped the kid and got sent to the headmistress, and we've been inseparable ever since. That first encounter turned out to be the template for our friendship. Ricky is, frankly, hopeless – always in trouble, he's clumsy, he's fat, he's forgetful. All-round useless. But he's also brilliant – he's really funny. I spend my life getting him out of scrapes, defending him and giving him somewhere to kip. But he makes me laugh like no one else. He's got a heart of gold and really cares for me. He'd take a bullet for me. I feel really bad writing this but he's become a problem. We do everything together. We're out every weekend. We're known everywhere as Dicky and Ricky, and the truth is, he wouldn't be that popular if it wasn't for me. He's a fair old liability and he's become a cock-blocker. We're both 18 now and I'd like to move on and go out with girls or at least be able to chat someone up without having to find a munter for Rick. I feel so disloyal saying this. I want him to be my best mate forever. If I get married, he'll be my best man. If I have kids, he can be a godfather to all of them. I just can't be responsible for his social life any more, and I can't have him putting the mockers on mine. How do I handle this?

Richard, Hull

You don't, Richard. All those years ago in the playground, you saved Ricky's life as surely as if you dived into a river and dragged him out. Everything he became afterwards was down to you. Save a man's life and you're responsible for that life. Ricky is a perfect sidekick – out of gratitude and friendship, he has remained a fat six-year-old for you – being funny, always showing you off in a good light by comparison to him. You could grow up to be a handsome, confident young man because another boy laid down his youth to give you that poise, confidence and *élan*. What Ricky did for you is one of the most touching and generous actions of selfless friendship. Who do you think really saved whom in that playground?

Dear Uncle,
Dick and I have been best mates all our lives. We do everything together. He's handsome, fit, athletic and suave, and I'm a bit of a joker and on the chubby side. And I've been happy to be like that for years. The thing is, now I realise I'm gay. And I don't know how to tell him. He'll think I'm coming on to him – he's a bit vain. But I'm really not – he's not my type. How can I break it to him that I can't spend every Friday and Saturday watching him pick up slappers in our filthy local? I've secretly started having sex with another guy we were at school with. He bit me on our first day. He says it was unresolved lust. Dick's going to be really hurt, bless him. But, anyway, I'd still like him to be my best man.

Ricky, Hull

Cheating is the most common subject of letters to this page. "Cheat" has two meanings: to break the rules of a game and to break the faith of a partnership. It's interesting that the second definition has grown from the first, and it implies that love is somehow a game. A game with rules. What's the only other thing that all games have? Winners and losers. So that rather implies that in love there is a winner, and presumably the winner is the most talented and skilled at it, and perhaps the luckiest. That may be what we mean by "lucky in love". But if you lose at love, more likely than not it's because the partner, or opponent, cheated, so cheating is actually the way to win. But that's obviously not right. So I'm going to merge all the letters into one, which is like cheating on a lot of people at once.

Let's kick off with Evangeline, who wrote simply to ask, "Is kissing cheating? My boyfriend says it is and if he ever caught me kissing another guy it would be grounds for throwing things – punches, vases, hissy fits, toys, prams – but, truthfully, I think that sometimes kissing's just a dance move." Evangeline has touched on what is the essence of cheating. If you think of love as being essentially naked rugby, then you need someone else to decide what's a forward pass and a high tackle. And what was just exuberant games-manship. Actually, when you're in love it does feel like naked rugby but then you're only allowed to tackle the same person over and over. Different people pull out a yellow card at different things.

Trevor for instance, who wrote last year and is probably in some sort of locked facility by now, asked me to back him up when he insisted that his girlfriend wore a full veil and chador when going to the pub. It was the pub bit that interested me: what was a conservative Muslim doing taking his girlfriend down the rub-a-dub? It turned out Trev was a practicing "don't know, don't care". He just thinks that veils are a really good idea and that, actually, preferably, girls should be kept in hessian sacks because they're all nympho bitches who'll blow tramps on park benches given half a chance. Bill Clinton from Washington famously didn't think that a blowjob was cheating, and Emma from Pinner says she feels cheated if she finds her husband masturbating. "That should be mine – all mine," she says. But Sylvie from Newcastle says she doesn't mind if Chuka has one off the wrist as long as he's thinking about her, which he swears, absolutely, on his life, he does every time. I would have printed photographs of Emma and Sylvie, which they included in their emails, but we couldn't have got anyone to advertise for the next three pages. There are men who think that prostitutes don't count as cheating or that having gay sex with strangers – as long as they're tops – counts as cheating.

Arnold, 75, wrote to say he'd just left Helen, his wife of 45 years, because he caught her holding hands with the octogenarian next door. He pointed out that sex had not been an issue, or indeed a possibility, for any of them for a decade, but that the intimacy of holding hands seemed to be the most terrible betrayal, adding that, if they'd been younger, they might have got over it with the thought of the years ahead of them, and that the memories might have been buried in time. "But realistically," he said, "we're down to the wire, and are unlikely to move on. There's nothing we can do to make it better." So he's off to an old people's home. This is the trouble with cheating: there are no acceptable rules, or laws. It could be a smile, or dancing to a song that you considered to be indefinably "ours". It can feel like cheating to go to a restaurant that you used to go to with someone else. Keeping photographs of exes can infuriate, like retrospective cheating. I don't have a definitive answer to any of this, but I would say that it is easier to work on your own jealousy than police somebody else's behaviour and thoughts.

The worst culprit for cheating is the mobile phone – sexting, texting. Most people who cheat do it on the phone, and they all get caught. My only piece of advice is that all of you consider every single text and Snapchat that you ever make as also being shared with your partner, because they all check your phones all the time – trust me on this one. And if you don't trust me, then trust yourself because you look at your girlfriend's texts when she goes to the bog like everyone else.

Here's a letter I got last week. It doesn't warrant or ask for a reply – it's just a story – but I thought you might like it. Bob had a row with his brother. A big row, in the course of which his brother told him that he was in fact the father of Bob's only child, a daughter, who is now 18. Bob is still married to his wife. He said the news was devastating. "I went for a walk. I came back after an hour and I sat my brother down, and quite calmly, I told him to consider who'd been cheated in this relationship. I'd had a daughter, who I'd shared Christmases and holidays, homework and bedtime stories with, who I taught to ride a bike and bought her first car, who brought her boyfriend home to see me. I had a wife, we'd made a life together, and a home. He'd had sex with someone else's wife but never managed to find one of his own, and he had a niece who thought he was a bit creepy. And he used to have a brother who looked up to him. Which one of us had life cheated?"

I'm fed up with waiting for you all to write to me with engaging and entertaining, thought-provoking problems. Why is it that young men think all problems begin and end with their penises? Yes, Derek, it is unnaturally small, but frankly that's the least of your worries. Go straight to the hospital for tropical diseases, your GP is not going to know what that is. And Thomas, thank you for that but I don't think "the guys" need to have the rules of "Is-it-cock-or-is-it-balls" explained to them, and your photographs weren't helpful or indeed printable so we've sent them to a specialist website with your email. Gregory, it shouldn't smell of anything. And certainly not the last days of the Roman Empire. The words "smell" and "genitalia" rarely sit happily within the same sentence. Few people have ever said, "Mmm, I love the smell of cock in the morning." Or, "D'you know, I really get homesick when I remember the smell of my sister's Friday night pants?" So just to break from your punningly insecure pud-pulling, I've decided to take some letters from famous philosophers. This one's from Friedrich Nietzsche in Germany:

Dear Sir,

Don't you think that the man of knowledge must be able not only to love his enemies but also to hate his friends? Don't bother replying, I already know the answer. I know the answer to everything. And whatever you say will only annoy me. Because if you're wrong, the answer will be bovine and stupid, and typical of the small-minded masses who don't deserve to exist. And if it's the right answer, it will be even more annoying because I will have to agree with you, which is plainly impossible for a man of my philosophical stature and perfect foresight. Nurse, nurse! Come quickly! I can't get the top off the bottle!

Friedrich, by email

Greetings, Friedrich. This is an interesting conundrum for young men, who are particularly attached to groups of friends, for whom belonging and loyalty attain a paramount importance. Young men tend to think that friendship transcends outside abstracts like right and wrong. Most young men wouldn't think twice about giving a friend a false alibi. Indeed the definition of friendship might be that you are prepared to lie for a mate, to take one for the team. There are effectively two moralities: the one that applies to everyone outside the gang and the one that applies only to those inside. Gang morality will always be seen as a higher

173

order than whatever it is the rest of the world lives by. But what you're talking about here is a third imperative, which is to be true to yourself and your knowledge despite everyone else, which I assume you mean as wisdom rather than merely facts. You need to be profoundly honest to give up merely personal animosity and attraction and you're plainly having a dig at your less clever thinker, Jesus Christ. But, of course, if you do love your enemies and hate your friends, you would simply invert your life and have a lot of mates you couldn't stand and a lot of enemies you were secretly fond of (which could be the definition of late middle-age.) I think the answer to your question, Freddie, is that you should be equally fond and critical of both friends and enemies and have a personal morality that you expect to apply only to yourself.

Dear Uncle Dysfunctional,
Freedom is what you do with what's been done to you.
Pick the bones out of that, you bourgeois apologist.

J-P Sartre, Paris

Thank you, Jean-Paul. Freedom is a concept that we very rarely ask to have explained. The young are particularly keen on freedom because they notice all the facets of it that they don't have. Their freedom is defined by the things that constrain it. Freedom is effectively understood to be not a thing but the absence of the obstacles to the thing: if you took away all the stuff that hemmed you in, then you'd be free. So, freedom is the absence of obstruction. But it is a quality that must by its very nature apply to everybody equally. Well, almost immediately your freedom is in mortal conflict with everyone else's. You can see that a world of complete freedom would be one of constant repression and restriction, a cacophony of argument, intensely dangerous and uncertain. The only freedom that is acceptable and workable is collective freedom, where we all agree to the maximum amount of liberty that can be allocated to each member of society to facilitate the greatest freedom of the whole. Most of this we organise ourselves. The bits we can't agree on we need governments to decide on our behalf.

But still, when you find yourself as free as you can be, when you leave the bespoke constraints of school, home and age, when you're old enough to have a job, to vote, free to make money, then you realise that actually your choices and desires are marked and limited by the things that have already been done to you by other people's freedoms. The way you've been brought up, the way that your parents and grandparents were brought up, how you were educated, the society you grew up in, what you have been exposed to and shielded from. Freedom isn't really delineated by the things that hem it in, but by your ability to envisage and utilise it. The greatest restriction of freedom is your fear and anxiety. There is in this the distinction between the freedom to and the freedom from: the freedom to keep slaves and the freedom from being a slave.

Thank you for that, Jean-Paul. And I'd like to pass on my favourite Sartre observation. You should say this out loud in a French accent, while having got up a photograph of Jean-Paul himself for the full benefit: "If I became a philosopher, if I so keenly sought this fame for which I'm still waiting, it's all been to seduce women, basically."

Dear Uncle Dysfunctional,

This may sound like an unusual problem – not the sort of thing that most blokes complain about – but my girlfriend is driving me mad, demanding sex. All the time. It's a balls-ache. Constantly, she's got her hands down my pants, and hers. "Come on, let's fuck: there's an R in the month," she says or, "It's St Priapus' Day" or, "Go down on me – Sheffield Wednesday just won."

"But you don't even support Wednesday," I say.

"I do if they get me off," she replies.

Whenever I try to put her off, or at least postpone it, she says I'm just intimidated by female sexuality and it's because she's behaving like an alpha male that I feel belittled. But that's not it. I just don't find it a turn-on. It's not sexy. It's boring. It's like constantly being told to take out the rubbish or go and fill the car with petrol – it's become a chore. I've just told her I've got a headache. It's so humiliating.

Tim, South Yorkshire

OK, Tim, you limp-dick little shag-dodger. Get back in there and make her beg for mercy. Munch and lunge till you make her eyes roll back in her head. Frot and rock till she's sitting on an ice pack, praying a mantra to the majesty of your testicles. Pound the crack of moan till she screams in tongues known only to charismatic Alabama churches. Cover her with the spume of love till she wants to start a business manufacturing scented candles that waft the beguiling odour of your sweaty taint. Pump her till she's feeling like a shelf of charity shop scatter cushions. Get a grip. Get some dick-bone. Clench your pelvic floor muscles. You're not just letting this bint goalkeeper off the hook or letting yourself down, you're letting every human with a pair down. Sex is a team game: them against us. If you dribble and dive under par, if you can't make the whole 90 minutes, you shouldn't be in the squad. Remember, sex is a game of two halves: the top half and the bottom half. There are winners and there are losers, and if you don't feel like a winner then you must be the other sort. And if you can't deliver a weeping multiple then get off the minge and let someone who's got the balls to do it have a go. So, Tim, go and knock one out in the bog, and consider your position as a man.

I don't actually believe any of that but I just wanted to know what it feels like to actually write it down. I wanted to stream my testosterone locker room. It was fun, but disgusting. Like eating a box of Krispy Kremes while watching Saudi Arabian porn: weird at the time but you feel like a seedy shit afterwards. Really seedy. Like budgerigar turds.

Your letter reminds me of another thing that happened a couple of weeks ago. The United States Food and Drug Administration agreed to license Flibanserin, or female Viagra (don't tell your girlfriend). There's a social and anthropological conundrum here: one of the main reasons for allowing a female sexual performance-enhancer to be prescribed was not for mechanical malfunction. Viagra and Cialis facilitate erections by increasing blood flow, and this new one does the same for women. But they don't need erections. And it's supposed to have a relaxing, uninhibiting mental element. But the real reason is that it's fair. If men can have a pill for sex, then so should women. Not licensing it would have been unfair. Even if it's not comparably necessary, it would have been sexist and discriminatory. You, more than anyone, will appreciate the irony of that.

These questions – of how much, who and the quality differential – are the meat and two veg, the missionary position, of agony columns. Almost every desperate enquiry boils down to: too little, too much, not good enough. And the answers are invariably touchy feely, like Liberal Party manifestos: love one another, talk to one another, sweat the details. And between you and me, it's all bollocks. Sex isn't about being a kind person. It's not a big generous sedative or gently charitable. Getting your rocks off is utterly me-centred. That's what makes it good. If sex were the exercise version of Red Nose Day, there would only be half a dozen people left in the world. It's not her demands of you that's the problem, it's your low expectations of yourself. It's not having too much sex, it's having too much mediocre sex. Mediocre, grudging sex. You don't like having sex with yourself because you're not very good at it. And you're not very good at it because you don't do enough of it. The way you get good at sex is the way you get good at everything: practice. Doing more, not less. But only doing the stuff that you really, really like. And tell your girlfriend to do the same. Last one to scream an expletive is a sissy.

Dear Uncle Dysfunctional,
It was my girlfriend's turn to choose the film. Last time, I took
her to see Mad Max: Fury Road, *which she said wasn't a proper*
date film. But it had loads of girl shit in it: pregnancy, romance,
tits. Anyway, she made me watch the cartoon movie about the
inside of some girl's head. What's all that about? I have no idea
why anyone would want to see this movie, or why they'd want
to show it to children. What's wrong with Ninja Turtles? But
my girlfriend loved it – sobbed a river and said I was a typical
man. And what's wrong with that? I've been aiming at typical
masculinity all my life.

Bryan, Knutsford

I feel your dude pain in a sort of lumpy, blokey way. By the
time your letter gets printed I expect they'll have launched
the sequel. For those of you – the single reader – who have
managed to avoid *Inside Out*, the premise is that our emotions
are run by emoticon homunculi: joy, sadness, disgust, anger
and then some other bloke who I didn't really make sense
of. Indecision or anxiety, or something. Anyway, as I had
to sit through it, to keep myself from punching the people
behind I tried to imagine the *Esquire* Uncle Dysfunctional
version of this movie. It would be about the two quite cute
little emoticons that live in your scrotum: The Ball Brothers,

The Testy Twins. Sort of Dumb and Dumber. Two young, working-class farm workers who spend their lives breeding and herding semen. They like their work and they care a lot about their sperm family. But the bane of their life is Dick Bellend, who lives next door. Every night, Dickie comes down and rustles the sperm, and every morning The Ball Brothers wake up and their flock has been shot into a sock. That Bellend is a proper wanker, a cocky bastard, and he's been getting above himself. So, together they start to work out how to make him fall in love, turn gay or become impotent. I can't work out which. It'll be a brilliant movie. I can see it now. The Bollock Brothers will be played by Matthew McConaughey and Tom Hardy. And Dickie Bellend is obviously Benedict Cumberbatch. There might be an opening for an arsehole, and I'm thinking Ray Winstone.

Dear Uncle Dysfunctional,
I just got into trouble for tweeting that my mate's mum looks
like a tranny. Now I've got to go into hiding.

George, Salford

You have fallen foul of the current nomenclature trend, George. This is serious. You need to keep up. You can't say, write or, indeed, think tranny any more. Tranny is a pejorative and derogative hate word, it is the sort of language that intimidates those in our society who are the most vulnerable: young men and women who feel that they have been mislabelled with the wrong ingredient. Just imagine how brave you have to be to tell your family, grandparents, school friends, the other members of the mosque, that you are, in fact, not the gender appearing on your Tinder account, but the opposite. Exactly. These people are in the most topsy-turvy, uncertain, vulnerable position it's possible for a human to find themselves in, and before they can realign their own jewellery requirements and genitals, they should be able to choose what they call themselves.

And, at the time of going to press, the accepted term is "trans", a trans-person. Now you may say, "Trans, tranny. Fuck it, what's the difference?" Well, it makes a difference to them. It's their name, they get to choose. So remember: it's trans. That's tranny with the little curly bit cut off the end.

Dear Uncle Dysfunctional,

I got my girlfriend pregnant when we were both 15. That was 17 years ago. My daughter's just brought home her boyfriend, who's two years older than I am. I think this is completely unacceptable. She says it's fine because she's nearly 18 and he's in his thirties, and it's not her fault that I was an underage child molester that got her mum up the duff (we're no longer together). And I take her point. But this is all sorts of creepy wrong. And he keeps calling me dad and laughing. And the worst thing is that we were at the same school, but obviously he was two years above me, and was a fucking bully.

Stanley, Jaywick

As *The Bible* says, "As you sow, so shall you pay child maintenance". The short answer is: you can't begin to have any say in who your children get off with. Unless that's an intrinsic part of your religion or culture, in which case obviously then that trumps love, sex and self-determination. The generally accepted algorithm for appropriate coupling is half the older partner's age plus seven. So, she's a bit off the reservation but not massively. You don't mention any of this guy's other qualities. Is he more successful than you? More socially adept? Is he better looking than you? I'm guessing that part of the problem is that he's not someone you can patronise or intimidate, which is an important part of the father–boyfriend relationship. On the other hand, marrying someone more successful than your father is an important social evolutionary step for a girl. What is strange is that if you asked your daughter if she would go out with a 15-year-old, she'd pull a face and say that's disgusting. Most girls see even a few years younger than them as unacceptable. But quite a lot older is perfectly agreeable. This is not an aesthetic or social choice. It's not because older men are better companions, are more sophisticated, are politer or have better conversation, or are more accomplished fornicators. It's a biological choice: they are more likely to be stable, established accomplished mates, and that will make them more trustworthy and adept fathers. You could look at your daughter bringing home a man of your age as being a compliment for your own record as a dad, which is more than could be said for her mother's choice of baby-daddy, and I bet her parents weren't at all thrilled when she came home with you.

Dear Uncle Dysfunctional,

My girlfriend's got the right hump. About a massage. She's packing bags, crying on the phone to her mum, swearing blue murder at me and, frankly, I can't make head nor arsehole of it. I like a bit of a rubdown. It relaxes me. I've got a high-stress job (better not ask), I like to have a bit of a schvitz and a stretch in the gym, a lounge in the hot fog, and then a bit of a deep-tissue pummel. There's a good girl at my gym and she always finishes me off in the correct and time-expected manner. And I've never thought anything about it. I mean, who doesn't get a happy ending? It's not even a thing. You bung her a tip and say, "Ta", and you feel great and smoothed out for a high-octane evening. How relaxed are you going to be with an angry stalk on? And who doesn't get a stiffy on the table? It's just another bit of your bod that needs de-stressing. Anyway, the girlfriend – I say the girlfriend, but we've been together for a couple of years and have got a sprog, and I think that she's it, give or take – she overheard me and a couple of mates having a bit of a natter about hand jobs, and she cornered me after and said, "Do you ever indulge?" And I said, "No, except for a polish after the massage." And she goes inter-fucking-galactic. "You're cheating on me and the kid, and you've been doing it all the time we've been together. I thought you loved me. I feel betrayed and humiliated. What am I going to tell little Taylor?" Bloody hell. I never saw this coming.

And the thing is, I'm as good as gold. I never play away from home. My dad was a dog and I remember what it put my dear mum through. Anyway, what can I say? This doesn't mean anything, right?

Alan, London

Well, yes and no Alan. We've covered cheating quite a lot here. But, apparently, your ever-alert penises have short memories. I sometimes imagine *Esquire* readers' penises as a troupe of bored meerkats all up on their hind legs, sniffing the air for juicy poon; never still, always questing with evil, ravenous, little beady smirks. And then I have to think about something else, like Buddhist sandpainting. The first point to make is that the definition of what is and isn't cheating is not down to the man in the dock. If you've been fouled, it isn't for the opposing team to say whether or not they were just playing the ball. If you've been robbed, it isn't for the dip to hold up his hands and say he didn't think you'd miss it. So, cheating is not what you can get away with. It's what she feels about what you get away with. And the truth is some partners roll their eyes at a hand job in a spa, and some partners shrug at a drunken gobble in a dressing room. But not many. And only if they're playing away themselves or they don't care that much about your knob one way or the other. The big question here is: would you feel as sanguine if she were doing it to you? Say, after a pedicure she got a generous fingering? Probably not. The thing with blokes and hand jobs is that they like to imagine they're closer to a wank than fornication, whereas girls don't even like to think about their boyfriends having one off the wrist on their own. The big deal is that it involves a third party. And now you have to ask yourself, does it matter who this third hand belongs to? I'm assuming your masseur is fit enough, but what if she were a 20-stone Bulgarian minger? What if she was a bloke? Would you be satisfied with a happy ending from a male masseur? I thought not. So, it's not just a mechanical relief, is it? Because the mechanic matters. And there's a telling anecdote about that. A shy cello player with a prominent symphony orchestra is on tour in the Far East. A horn player tells him that, if he fancies it, there's a really good massage parlour next to the hotel. Never having done anything like this, the cellist nervously books in for an hour's relaxing stroke. The masseur's only done one leg when he's sporting an expectant stiffy like a drumstick, and she smiles and winks and says, "Would you like a wank, soldier?" "Oh, well, actually, yes. I would rather," says the cellist. "OK," she replies, going to the door, "I'll be back in five minutes when you've finished."

You see, if it wasn't a thing, as you put it, you could always have seen to yourself. But the real point is that she cares. You would mind far more if she didn't. A lot of loving someone is protecting them from the vulnerability of their love. You had a duty not to let the mother of your child be hurt by her love for you. And if that twinges with guilt, well it's not due to a sordid tug in the gym, it's because you've failed at the first job of being in love, which is to make the person who offers their love back feel safe.

Let us pause a moment and remember the humble hand job, the Cinderella of sexual congress all too often overlooked and unconsidered compared to its two noisier, messier and more demanding sisters, the gobble and the hump. The tug is always thought of as being second best, a consolation prize, a brush off, when in fact it is a thing of skill and beauty – the sex act with the most dexterous control, and prestidigitatious possibilities. A skilled, hand-crafted rub-a-dub-dub can keep the recipient on the agonising edge of a mission for minutes, and the ability to tease the *moment critique* is a highly sought-after skill. A hand job can either be a helter-skelter spin, a mad dash of emetic exuberance, or a slow torture of postponed pleasure. It is the drum solo of the concept album and, in the hands of a master, a thing of divine and agonising beauty. Don't think of the assisted wank as either humble or negligible. In the right hands, it is the epilepsy of heaven.

Over the years, we at *Esquire* have collected a short spankography of the unlikely and inappropriate places that people – girls and boys – have been asked to offer hand relief. Laura says she was once asked to toss off an ex-boyfriend in a graveyard at the funeral of his father because he was so sad. And then asked to make it a blow job because his dead dad would have wanted it that way. There are a lot of requests for hand jobs in churches during services, obviously a lot at weddings, and Julie says that she was asked for a crafty tug by the best man because he was so turned on by her frock; she was the bride.

Sarah says she got drunk and took numerous pills and mind-altering herbs to settle her nerves at her new posh boyfriend's family black-tie dinner in a stately home, but got confused, and stuck her hand down the thigh of her beau's father. When she tried to retrieve the situation, he grabbed her wrist, rearranged his napkin, and winked. James (not his real name) says he gave manual relief to an aged but still fit Lord during the Queen's Speech in the Palace of Westminster.

Grahame's mother says that at her Grahame's 10th birthday party, a little lad came into the kitchen and pulled down his shorts to reveal a keen, buoyant little pee pee. The lad said that Grahame had said that his mum would give him a hand with it. She said firmly that she couldn't, but told him that if anyone more than twice his age ever touched the boy's willy, it would turn blue and grow curly like a pig's tail. Which, incidentally, is true.

Dear Adrian,

I know this sounds funny, as in amusing, but that's why I'm reduced to writing to you about it. No one will take me seriously and, consequently, I suffer from nervous flatulence. I produce a lot of wind and release it at really inconvenient moments in lifts, and I have an overwhelming need to fart whenever I have a massage. I can feel the gasses building up, and the pressure on my sphincter is unbearable. If there is a quiet moment in the theatre or at a concert, my bottom can sense it and is compelled to fill the unforgiving silence with a rumble of gastric crowing. I can fart rhythmically as I walk, each footfall producing a martial trump. I rarely get to have sex with the same person twice as each thrust is accompanied by a sphincter whistle; an orgasm is a raga of ecstatic ululation. I have tried everything to hush my cacophonous bowel: I eat a bland and blameless diet; I take Friendly Flora and gallons of Milk of Magnesia. But it makes no difference. Whenever the mood is sombre, solemn or seductive, my arse bellows like a drunken mariachi band. In desperation, I've even attempted to alter the pitch of my sphincter by changing its aperture using a selection of blunt objects of increasing width in the hope that it might become more of a "futt" than a "parp", but to no avail.

Please, please could you take this seriously and tell me what I should do?

Charlie, Windermere

Get a dog. Get two dogs.

Dear Uncle Dysfunctional,
You're good at using your words. Can you recommend any sure-
fire, killer pick-up lines?

Ahmed, Hong Kong

Yes: silence. And a fleeting smile. There are no sure-fire
pick-up lines. Pick-up lines are a wholly male myth. Nothing
you say – nothing slick, funny, provocative, winsome, disingenuous, pleading – is going to make any girl have sex with
you. Nothing, ever. I mean it. If you say, "Have you got
any Jewish in you? Would you like some?" And a girl you've
never met before says, "mazel tov" it's because she fancied
you before you opened your mouth, and she decided to get
her end away despite your arthritic *bon mot*. The golden rule
of sex that all men should understand, indeed, most men
should have tattooed, is that you get laid despite your best
efforts, not because of them. And the dominant partner in
any social arrangement is the one who has the power of
veto and holds the goods. And that'll be the ladies.

❖   ❖   ❖

Dear Mr Gill,

I used to work as an escort. I come from a poor family. My father was, well, let's just say he was a man. I was a student, I needed the money. It was all quite polite and provincial: business dinners, company awards dos, lonely travelling salesmen and, yes, I had sex with them, but lying underneath them was far less stressful than sitting opposite them in four-star hotel dining rooms. Anyway, I gave it up when I got my first job. I'm a strategy advisor for small businesses in the retail sector. I don't feel any shame about it. What I did was a means to an end. And now I've fallen in love – with an amazing boy who's a couple of years younger than me. We get on, he's good to me, we've moved in together. He's a committed political activist with a big heart, big dreams and quite a big cock. He does great things for me and will do great things for the country. He's going to fight a winnable seat at the next election. He doesn't have much to do with his parents, though – he and his father don't see eye-to-eye. Anyway, his dad came to visit and guess what? He was a client. And he remembers me. He didn't say anything, it was in his eyes. He came back the next day when my lad was out and told me that I had to break up the relationship as it would ruin his son's political career when my past came out, as undoubtedly it would. He knew his son was in love with me and would never go of his own accord, so if I loved him I must set him free. And then he left, saying he knew that I was a good and decent woman, and that was the person he was appealing to. I was distraught. I've only ever been in love once, and I will only ever be in love once. What neither my darling boy nor his father know, nor anyone else, is that I have a congenital weakness – an inherited condition. It's been dormant but now it's not and I will die of it, sooner rather than later. And the end will be painful, slow and incapacitating. Must I face this alone, in despair? If I tell my boyfriend he will never leave me, but must I send him away? Completely cut our lives apart? Is our mutual misery the right thing to do? Is this the final act of truly selfless love?

Violetta, Royal Leamington Spa

I've been waiting for 40 years to answer this letter, Violetta, which is the mother of all agony. It is the ultimate agony. So, the conventional wisdom says that you have to let him go, as you intuit. It is the ultimate proof of love. It also means you pass the fragile butterfly of devotion onto him because when he discovers that you have a fatal condition (sorry, by the way – that's a bummer), he then has to exercise his obligation to the courage of love, and give up his career to come back to you. This will naturally be too little and too late, and you will die and he'll be bereft, and that is the tragedy of love as the two great agony aunts of the 19th century, Dumas fils and Verdi, saw it. It's hard to argue with them. But now we don't have to be tied to the connections and the moral rigidity of the past. We can ask, what would Richard Curtis do?

OK, obviously you have to break up with him, but you know he loves you too much to go on his own. You must make him break up with you by turning up at some public event, probably a school play, with another man. This could be the good-looking but closeted gay older man next door. The boyfriend will see you, be mortified, break up, and prepare to leave the country to go and work for a charity in the Far East. In the meantime, you will weep on the shoulder of the old man neighbour, who will turn out to be a retired/struck-off consultant who notices the telltale symptoms of your hereditary fatal condition, but, by further chance, he will also be the world expert on said condition and he knows that it is curable if caught in time. But, apparently, you only have 12 hours left to get the miracle cure from a cottage hospital somewhere in remote Scotland. The only person who can get you there is the boyfriend's father in his helicopter. After a tearful confrontation, he flies you to Scotland, where a strange and eccentric nurse played, I think, by Eddie Redmayne, administers the cure by enema. Then you have to rush back to London, and sprint to Heathrow to head off the boyfriend at the gate.

But, here's the final twist: while the loudspeaker plays "Fly Me to the Moon" you miss him, just by a moment. Too late: the security guards catch you. But with the help of an enigmatic Rowan Atkinson, you give them the slip. You disguise yourself as an air hostess and smuggle yourself on-board, publicly declaring your love, and health, while giving the safety demonstration. The cabin erupts into applause and, by chance, there's a brass brand sitting in economy to play Herb Alpert's "This Guy's in Love with You". It turns out that the captain of an airliner is like the captain of a ship, and he can marry you. The wedding reception is chicken or beef from the trolley. And Stephen

Fry, who just happens to be travelling in first class, agrees to give the best man's speech over the tannoy. It's the best best man's speech ever. You honeymoon on a deserted tropical island in the Indian Ocean.

You see, that's the real, 21st century-inclusive, two fingers to misery, give us a romantic soft-centred ending. It is the endorphin of reassurance that everything will be all right. So, fuck you Alexandre Dumas fils, and up yours Giuseppe Verdi (or Joe Green as you'd have been known in Camden Town).

Of course, the addendum, if you're thinking of rewriting this as a script for Danny Boyle: just at the end of the best man's speech when Fry says, "Raise your glasses to the bride and groom," a bloke at the back shouts, "Allahu Akbar!" and everything goes white. And then you hear the disembodied voice from the beginning of *Love Actually*, which goes on about all the people who died in the Twin Towers and their last messages not being about hate but love, but sort of ironic. Except it isn't ironic. Love does transcend everything. Which is the original message of *La Dame aux Camélias* and *La Traviata*. But there's no reason why there shouldn't be a happy ending as well. The damnedest saying of all your granny's dim sayings is, "It's better to have loved and lost than never to have loved at all." No one who ever loved and lost would say that. It's better to have loved and won than anything else. Being in love and losing it is worse than anything else – worse than bereavement, worse than cancer, worse than being beaten 4–0 by Hull.

197

Dear Uncle Dysfunctional,
I've got this problem. A few years ago, I was working for the
UN in refugee camps in the Middle East and there was a girl.
She was on her own, desperate and pretty. And she was great,
it was great. I helped a bit. Made sure she was safe. Got her
some medical treatment, a coat, and one thing led to another
and we started having a fling. It was sort of secret. Because,
you know, they don't really approve of humping the patients.
This was different. Really. We were close. She was beautiful
and gentle and understandably needy. I suppose if I'm honest,
in retrospect, she had more invested in the relationship than
I did. But we knew it was always going to be limited, or I
assumed we knew. After six months, I was moved back to
Geneva and then to London and I fell in love and got married
to a brilliant human rights lawyer. We'd been doing IVF,
though without much success. And then – this was five years
later – I got a call from a refugee detention centre in London.
They said they had my son with his mother. Fuck me. I had
no idea that there'd been a child. I'd heard nothing. I had to
tell my wife. She was upset, obviously. Actually, she was morti-
fied. Even though it all happened before I ever met her it was
the thought of the child. He's five now. She's a really good
woman, my wife. She said we should adopt him, give him a

home. A future. What do you think I should do?
                              Name and address withheld

How nice to hear from you, Mr Pinkerton. I'd been hoping
you'd write. You've quite a reputation. I think it's fair to
say you must be the most universally, comprehensively
loathed and despised man in all of opera. There can be
barely any bloke who has sat in the stalls and not thought,
"Give me five minutes alone with that bastard and I'd teach
him a lesson." For the reader who has never quite got round
to seeing *Madam Butterfly*, let me explain briefly how this
pans out. Your ex-girlfriend waits and waits for you to come
back to her and your child, never doubting your love, until
she sees your wife and is forced to realise that the only
thing she has – her son – will have a better life with your
wife and you. To make that happen, she kills herself. In
one of the most coruscating, desperate and shocking scenes
ever made up, more distressing than any horror movie,
Butterfly plays blind man's bluff with her little boy and
while he is blindfolded and searching for her she silently
kills herself. The boy is discovered by his father. But we're
not going to let that happen, Mr Pinkerton. We're going
to apply this column's patented Richard Curtis Retrospective
Happy Ending.

So here's how it goes. You get the call that your ex-girlfriend
and her son are going to be deported. You feel sad in a
self-pitying sort of way, and say there's nothing you can do
about it. Crack open a beer, because you need a drink, and
turn on the football. Your wife hears this tinkling sound. It's
the scales falling from her eyes. She sees you for the callous,

lazy, self-interested, opportunistic little shit you are. She jumps in the car and gets to the detention centre where your son and his mother are being led out to be sent back to the hellhole they escaped from. The mother is secretly preparing to kill herself. Your wife, the lawyer, says she is going to act on Butterfly's behalf. She asks to interview her in private. And something miraculous happens. At the lowest ebb of both their lives, they look into each other's eyes and realise fate has brought them to this moment. One with a child but no security, the other desperate to be a parent. Their mutual need leads to love. Your wife gets them out of jail, they set up home together, she divorces you, takes half your money and the house, Butterfly sues you for child support, and takes the other half. They get married in a small church in Gloucestershire and the little lad sings "All You Need is Love". No one dies. Not a dry eye in the universe, except yours.

Now, for the rest of you this should be instructive. You need to understand why Pinkerton is such a compellingly ghastly character. He's not evil, or particularly cruel, or a psychopath. He's just selfish, expedient and cowardly. He's so shocking because he's so very close to all of us. It only takes a couple of degrees of moral laziness, a weakness of resolve, a little self-indulgence and we could all be Pinkerton. And that's what makes him such a repellent character. The cartoon monsters – the Rippers and Hitlers – are miles away. Pinkerton is just a bad hair day away. When Puccini wrote *Madam Butterfly*, his lyricist pointed out that the tenor playing Pinkerton would have to be a big star, and that would be expensive. But he didn't have anything to sing in the third act, and that would be a waste. Why not write him an aria, maestro? Because, said Puccini, with great Italian emotion, he doesn't deserve one.

Dear Uncle Dysfunctional,

I'm a woman in my forties and I've decided to become celibate. I'm giving up sex, with the exception of the occasional comfort frot. It's not that I don't like sex or that sex has given up on me. There's no shortage of men who'd jump aboard given half a chance. It's just I can't be bothered any more. I can't be bothered with the preparation, the dressing up, the depilation, the trying to see my bottom in the mirror, all the humiliating business that goes with sex, the time and the emotion invested in even a half-hearted affair. As I get older, I'm less willing to put up with the neediness, the selfishness and the insecurity of men with no clothes on. I've realised that dressed men are really perfectly nice, and if there's no question of sex they behave like grown-ups and turn out to be interesting and funny, dependable and kind. While the men you're fucking rarely are. And much as I've enjoyed sex in the past, I don't think that the intense fleeting pleasure is worth all the tedious hard work of the prelude and the aftermath. And I've discovered there are an awful lot of other women like me. I just thought you'd like to know.

Violet, Cobham

I think you're right. I meet more and more grown-up women who aren't interested in having sex with me. When asked if he still had sex, Sophocles replied, "I am only too glad to be

202

free of all that; it is like escaping from bondage to a raging madman." All sexual relations happen between three people: two lovers and a raging madman. I've been thinking for some time that there should be a variation of Tinder for people who don't want to have sex any more. You can flick left for uninterested and right for can't be bothered. It would be enormously gratifying and a source of quiet stress relief.

Dear You,

I always rim a fella when I'm giving him a blow job. I mentioned this to a group of my girlfriends. They were all disgusted, saying they'd never stick their tongue up some bloke's arse on the first date. Do you have a ruling on this?

Rose, via email

No. But I can pass on an old posh prostitute's trick. You won't be surprised by how many men ask for rimming from hookers because, obviously, you go out for what you're not getting at home. And the brasses charge extra for it. The trick is to get the john into the doggy pillow-biting position – arse upwards – then spread the cheeks, make complimentary and delicious remarks about the presented sphincter, and then stroke and tease it with the pad of a finger, avoiding oral-rectal contact. Very few heterosexual men can tell the difference between a tongue and a finger without seeing it, so the sex worker gets her extra, the bloke gets his jollies, and no one gets giardia.

Dear Sir,

I've been perusing your effulgent errs for some time with, I must declare, a vanishing pleasure. What was once engorged is now flaccid. When you write about the straightforward mechanics of congress between honest working people, overcome as they may be with inappropriate lust and an abundance of blameless ardour, then oft your replies are useful, passing lyrical, perchance antic with bouquets of heavenly smut. I particularly remember with ribald amusement your injunction on how to delicately cope with rectal effluvia after anal sex in polite company. It had an earthy practicality. And the hilarity of your instructions for plaiting a fairy garland into a harvest festival was a boon for aesthetic spinsters blessed with an artistic bent. But I must tell you, my patience runs thin over all this mawkish sentimentalising about opera plots. Fat, warbling women, freaking with spittle-fleck, lust after fatter, pederastic gentlemen mostly from headier climes. It's not the sort of useful instruction that the hard-working denizens of Dorset need, or indeed wish to know. I hope, Mr Dysfunctional – I demur to name you uncle, you are no kin of mine – that you should offer the experience of your priapic pen that drips the unction of solicitous communion into the ears of simple souls desirous of carnal equilibrium. Take, for instance, my own particular canny conundrum in the fanny-filling department. There was a chap, a shepherd, who was passing interested in introducing his trouser ram to my sheep dip. But then his dog drove his ewes off a cliff. And that's not a euphemism. Sadly, he now finds himself in straightened circumstances – though not in the man sausage area. And then there is the old gent up the road, who simply adores me and wants to be married, but I don't sense there's any capering round his maypole, no top C in his choir. He is, in short, a gangling shagdodger, though he does have his own linen and fine parlour ornaments. I suppose I could marry him and continue ploughing my own furrow, but then there's the army officer – tight breeches, with a pert motte-and-bailey. He jerked his sword from his scabbard and lunged at my face. I almost swooned with the excitement as he flashed within centimetres of my quivering lip. I could smell the martial musk on his manly musket. What shall I do? My South Downs have got bloat, and I desperately need someone with a firm hand to relieve them.

Bathsheba, Dorset

Bathsheba, how good to finally hear from you. Of course, we already know your story: you are the heroine of *Far from the Madding Crowd*, a capricious, contrary little bitch, who makes the shepherd Gabriel Oak's life a misery; you humiliate Farmer Whatshisname by sending him love letters as a joke; you trap Sergeant Troy, who really loves someone else, so that Farmer Whatsit shoots the soldier dead and gets locked up for the rest of his life. So you have to reluctantly do with what's left: the miserable shepherd, who's now your hireling. And that's the end of the book. Except we all know that you're going to go on to make his life a slow, rural misery as well. You're often held up as being a bit of a proto-feminist, a role model, as a girl who wants to remain independent but also has needs in a masculine world. Well, up to a point. Actually, you're a bit of a prick-tease and want the men around when there's a haystack on fire or the sheep need de-farting, but then it's "push off and mind your own business" when they fancy a hand job.

So, we can apply Richard Curtis' algorithm to this story. For a start, Gabriel Oak, the shepherd (played by Martin Clunes), gets a better dog, probably played by the one who won *Britain's Got Talent*. Then his sheep aren't driven off a cliff and he's not bankrupted. Then Sergeant Troy (Cillian Murphy) the sword-swaggerer's great love, the maid, will be miraculously saved from dying in childbirth by said Gabriel Oak who is a natural healer/vet/midwife character. Troy will gratefully marry the mother of his lovechild and becomes best friends with Oak. He leaves the army and they set up a sheepskin coat business together. Farmer Thingy (Kenneth Branagh) realises that in fact he doesn't need a woman at all, and takes on a Polish handyman to see to his needs. And I'm afraid, Bathsheba, that leaves you where you belong – on your own, with all your judgements and complaining. But actually, I think you can find solace in writing a weekly column for the *Mail on Sunday* about the funny things that happen in rural life and what dreadful, unappreciative and boorishly thankless bastards men are.

Mon cher Oncle Dysfu,

Apologize! My English is extraordinary. I have a monumental wife catastrophe. I love Emma with a passion, ardour and panache that will be impossible for the cold, Anglo-Saxon heart to comprehend. She is mon lune et étoiles. *I am not a confident* homme. *I was a discreet infant, also a shy student of illness. Feminine learning was not contagious for me. But then Emma comes to my lap, as you say, and my life is engorged. We are a small country doctor in a little bourgeois ville. It is too petite for my Emma. I worry that she may be offering her discreet vagina to afternoon scoundrels. I am at my amusing aperçu's end and I have a patient with a disingenuous foot. Can you console?*

Charles, Normandy

I feel your pain. All men who have heard your story will have felt a little twinge of identification. You are the sorry dupe in the greatest tragic anti-romance of all literature. You are a country doctor who lacks confidence, excitement, personality or competence. So, just like the rest of us really. And you can't believe your luck when Emma agrees to marry you in an absurdly elaborate wedding that promises a sybaritic life of luxury and social advancement. And you're right – you shouldn't have believed it. She is vivacious, impulsive, romantic, coquettish, impossible, contrary, passionate and fickle. And very expensive. So, just like the women we all fall in love with, really. In fact, for us Anglos, *Madame Bovary* encapsulates all our prejudices about the French. The extraordinary thing about this book is that even though you are the blameless victim and your wife is a cheating puta, we are forced to feel empathy for her and a bored derision for you. Emma goes on and has a couple of affairs. She has a daughter that she neglects. She borrows money you can never pay back. And, finally, when it all unravels, she takes arsenic and dies in agony. You, being a clod-hopping chump, still think she is perfect and give her a funeral as elaborate as your wedding. And then you have to sell everything to pay off her debts. Finally, you discover the letters that prove she'd been taking her love to town, in a big way, and you become a recluse and die in the garden. Your daughter, Berthe – even her name shows how unloved she was – is sent to work in a factory, the final tragic nail, as so much of this story is about keeping up with the Dubois. So, Charles, I wish I could tell you that this can all be fixed with a bunch of garage carnations, a back rub and a week-end's glamping. But it can't. However, we can apply the patented Richard Curtis algorithm to your story and see if the maestro's happy endings are a match for Monsieur Flaubert. As you might expect, the answer is all about her and very little to do with you.

Madame Bovary is a tragic heroine because she has such huge expectations and dreams for her life but the only avenue open to realise them is through a propitious marriage and motherhood, and when these things fail her, she takes the desperate and predictable medication of sex and shopping. She is a woman stifled and cuffed to the restrictions and conventions, and probity, of her time. But with the wand of Richard Curtis we can fix that. Not by changing the plot, as there is nothing in the character or potential of either you or her that can make a difference, and no amount of cash will undo the arsenic. But we simply change the time. Make *Madame Bovary* contemporary. We can do that now. Suddenly, there are far fewer social restrictions, far more options. Emma really ought to be in show business, and she ought to be in America. She yearns to be a celebrity so, with the new, improved Curtis version, she'll be played by Beyoncé and living in California. Her fame will be kicked off by an internet sex tape. She'll have a string of film-star lovers before settling into a cable reality show. She'll have her own line in underwear, mime a pop song and set up a charity for orphaned miniature dogs. She will finally marry a Florida cosmetic surgeon, played by Jon Hamm. She will adopt a number of multicultural children and live publicly in the unrelenting glare of celebrity, which is what Emma wanted all along. You, of course, will probably remain miserable, and a cuckold. And finally, Charles, lay off the unfortunate with the club foot: like everything else in your life, it's not going to turn out well.

Dear Uncle Dysfunctional,
Am I normal?

Trevor, New York

No one normal would ever ask that question, Trevor. The definition of normal is not wondering what normal is. Normal isn't a thing. It's an absence of things. Mostly odd things. It is odd to ask if you're normal. So, the answer is no. If it's any consolation, it's also odd to write letters to strangers passing judgements on their normality.

Dearest Unc,

My girlfriend is up the duff. It wasn't planned but we're thrilled. Thing is, we've just had a scan and it's fucking triplets. Oh my God, three of them. And all boys. She's in shock. Spends her whole time laughing and then crying. I'm trying to be practical, concentrate on the important shit like, obviously, what are we going to call them? She wants Athos, Porthos and Aramis (she did A-levels). That sounds like a fucking perfume shop. I said, "Absolutely no way." So then she said Plácido, José and Luciano. I'm from Hull, not fucking Rimini. Apparently, they're opera singers. The kids'll be fat knicker-sniffers, bellowing "just one Cornetto". No. Absolutely not. No Johnny Foreigner names. We've had Brexit – they'll get deported. So she sobs for a bit and says, "I've got it: Robin, Maurice, Barry." Fucking fuckety fuck, fuck, shit the bed. She wants to give birth to The Bee Gees. "Oh, but Saturday Night Fever's *my favourite film," she sobs. "And 'Stayin' Alive' is such a hopeful theme to play in the delivery room for giving birth to triplets. It's the harmonies." She can't think straight, obviously. They'll be born with rabbit teeth and ridiculous hair. "No, OK," she howls, "you choose." Well, I've thought about it, and I've got fucking brilliant names – worth having triplets for. Almost worth living with my fucking mentalist girlfriend for. OK, are you ready? Clint, Lee and Eli. Eastwood, Van Cleef and Wallach. Get it? Oh, come on. The*

Good, the Bad and the Ugly. It's genius. They'd go to parties dressed as cowboys: "I'm the good one, he's the ugly one, he's the bad one." That's a gag that keeps on giving, that will never not be funny; at passport control, school registers, magistrates' court. Clint, Lee, Eli. She's just run out of the room and locked herself in the bog. I don't know what the matter with her is. That is the single, or rather triple-best idea I've ever, ever had. (After forgetting that the condom was in my other jeans.) It's so good, I had to write to tell you. Can you help? Can you improve? And don't say Groucho, Harpo and Chico – I'm not having them circumcised.

Jules, by email

There was a fat prat who begat,
Bloke triplets named Nat, Tat and Pat.
It was fun in the breeding, but hell in the feeding,
There wasn't a spare tit for Tat.

Dearest Uncle,

I'm a neutrois person, sometimes identifying as "a gender".
Though people always ask, "What's next on the agenda?" And
laugh, like they're the only person who's ever said it. And I either
have to gender shame them and walk out, or just smile and
pretend I've never heard it before. The thing is, my partner is
gender fluid. Although, actually, ze is being a bit sluggish at the
moment. The fluidity gets stuck in the blokey quadrant when it
comes to tidying up and folding things. What is it about the Y
chromosome that means you can't fold a towel? OK, that's not
what I'm writing about. I'm comfortable with my self-identifi-
cation, and I'm basically happy with my gender-sluggish mate,
but what I can't stand is not being able to have a conversation
about anything else. It's all my cis friends talk about to me. In
fact, all my LGBTQ friends talk about it endlessly. It's not that
I'm not interested, up to a point, in gender, it's that we all have
to be so careful and polite and worried about saying the wrong
word. It's like talking about sex in church. Did you know, there
are more than 50 gender identifications? You need to be a genital
trainspotter to get them all right. What, for instance, are
"spicvak pronouns", for fuck's sake? Or "two-spirited"? Actually,
that's quite interesting: it's a Native American (not Indian) Zuni
term for someone who swings both ways. It's called "he man eh"
in Cheyenne, which sounds funny in English but, of course, you

can't laugh because that's transgender-shaming someone's sensibilities. And it's white colonial insensitivity, humour hegemony. I'm fed up with having to pussyfoot around all this stuff. And, of course, you can't say "pussyfoot" because that offends absolutely everybody, including foot fetishists. I'm all in favour of political gender correctness – safe spaces, non-discriminatory language – but it all becomes about the grammar and finger-wagging snobbery. It's not like being free and open and just what you like, it's like being a member of some terrible, stuffy club. And it's not about the really important stuff, like housing and benefits and schools and job discrimination and what's on your passport. There is no end to the language and the pronouns, and it's become my identity when my whole fight was to lose my identity. I'd like to talk about football and Game of Thrones, *and Theresa May's kitten heels, and quinoa. Anything but gender definitions. The only thing I envy about all you cis folk is that you never talk about it, your gender. It's like the colour of your front doors – just there. Whether you cook on gas or electric, full fat or diet; it's what you are. I want to be like that. Do you know what the definition of a bio queen is, by the way? It's a person who identifies as a woman, dressing as a man who dresses as a woman. For fuck's sake, which communal dressing room do they use?'*

E., London

There was a non-binary neutrois from Khartoum,
Who took a gender neutral ace to ze room.
They argued all night, about who had the right,
To name what and which and then whom.

Mr Dysfunctional,

Oh boy! Ohhhhhh boy. Are we great. Are we great. We put the "grrrr" in great. The grrrrrrrrrrrrr. And the "eat". We put the "eat" in great: breakfast with syrup and butter and hash browns on the side. Liberals don't do that – they don't have butter dripping off their chins at the bar, listening to Tammy and crying into their first Jack at 8.30 in the morning. They have kale juice and Valium on the side. Grrrrrrr give yourself a big hug – a manly, A-frame, "no downstairs touching" hug. Oooo yeah, you've earned that. Unless, of course, it's a little intern beside you. Then you can give her the loin lunge because you've earned that, too. You are president. Oh yes. You are "this isn't about me, this is all us – all us." You are president. Who put the "dent" in president? You did. No, I did. We all did. We all loin-lunged the "dent" in president. But only the guys – only the guys with a functioning, low-hanging, unfeasibly juicy pair are president. Sorry ladies, no president for you. You're squashed on the glass ceiling like a damselfly on the windscreen of life. Oh my God, who writes this stuff?

But the pussy-grab you can feel, ladies, that's exciting. A fistful of man digit – it belongs to a president. Sweet. Heat. Suck it up. When I say "it doesn't mean just me, of course", I am the President of Presidents. I am The Trumpster, the Grand Wizard of Trump. OK. Grrrrrrrrrr. Incredible. Incredible!

I would just like mention the Secret Service here today: if there's someone beside you who you can't see, a big, all-American man-mountain, he's in the service – of the secrets. They're not presidents, they're better than that – they look after presidents who are better than all the other presidents. The man who saves the president's life on a daily, hourly, minutely, secondly basis, that's who. I've met some of the most powerful, attractive, fanciable, fecund men ever in the Secret Service. They're incredible. Who put the "in" in incredible? Whenever we have a shower in the morning, and we're all under the power together, I can feel the man-power, and smell the most real men, with the most real jobs in the real world. Four-square, hands on hips, clench-it-and-take-it-like-a-man jobs.

I have a question. It's not that I don't know the answer, it's what liberals call rhetorical. Yes, they do say "rhetorical" because they can't say "rest your tonsils on that, bitch". It's a question where I already know the happy ending. Pay attention, Dysfunctional. Who put the "dys" in dysfunctional? Don't tell me, I already know. So, the question is this: me and my buddies here have got to be president for at least four years. Really. I've had marriages that haven't lasted that long. So my question is, Dysfunctional, I've got to deal with a shedload of other countries. None of them are America. And just why is this? At this juncture of our history, why aren't there more Americas?

I mean, why aren't we franchising America? Buying up useless countries, asset-stripping them down and rebranding them as America? This is the problem with Washington – no one has a business mind. No one thinks outside of the diplomatic box.

So, this is what we're doing: we're going to franchise until we

217

have the biggest damn takeaway country in the world. And then
we're going to start building American worlds in space. Oh yes.
USA! USA! USA! The question is, I need to meet all these other,
un-American countries and, like, smack them, or pussy-grab
them, but I'm damned if I can tell them apart. So, can you give
me a handy guide to telling countries apart? For instance, if
they were say, like, Miss World contestants, which, obviously
they all are, but didn't have the sash because I'd already used it
to blindfold them so the Secret Service guys could get their balls
buffed without having to be seen. If countries were pussy, what
sort of pussy would they be? This is your assignment. Who put
the "ass" in assignment? You know it, baby. Go work it.

Donald, Washington, D.C.

Your letter came as something of a surprise, Mr President
Trump. I didn't have you down as someone who asked for
advice, though I did imagine that you would write letters
as though you were addressing a Nuremberg rally of drunk,
antique gun enthusiasts. Your enquiry raises an interesting
question: are countries like women? Can you anthropomor-
phise them? The fact that most people do see their nation
as a person is interesting, and that most of us tend to see
her as a woman, usually a mother. I mention this because
of your observation about glass ceilings: you may not have
a woman president but you already live in a female country.
It is a woman, it is a mother, it is the motherland. You have
never lived in a male country. America is personified by a
woman: Liberty. She stands at the end of your hometown,
adorned with a poem by another woman asking for the
world to send her refugees. Liberty was given to America

by the French, and she bears some familiar resemblance to their national figure, Marianne, the revolutionary feminist with her breasts out, storming the barricades. In Britain, we have Britannia, a seafaring goddess who harks back to classical Rome. The Romans had any number of representative women, as did the Greeks. And the Egyptians. So if you want to remember nations by their female familiars, there's Marianne, Britannia, Athena, Liberty, and you might like the she-wolf of Rome for America.

Acknowledgements

Alex Bilmes would like to thank Nicola Formby, Gerald Scarfe, Jamie Byng, Hannah Knowles, Rafi Romaya, Ed Victor, the staff of British *Esquire*, especially Rachel Fellows and Brendan Fitzgerald, and Adrian, the Uncle I never knew I wanted, but am lucky to have had.